The setting for the Michael Todd production of "January Thaw."

"JANUARY THAW"

BY

WILLIAM ROOS

BASED UPON THE NOVEL BY

BELLAMY PARTRIDGE

THE DRAMATIC PUBLISHING COMPANY

CHICAGO

"JANUARY THAW"

COPYRIGHT, 1945, BY WILLIAM ROOS
COPYRIGHT, 1946, BY WILLIAM ROOS

BASED UPON THE NOVEL, "JANUARY THAW,"
BY BELLAMY PARTRIDGE

All Rights Reserved

PRINTED IN THE UNITED STATES OF AMERICA

Copy of the program of "January Thaw," as produced at the
Golden Theatre, New York, February 5, 1946.

MICHAEL TODD

presents

"January Thaw"

by William Roos, adapted from the
novel by Bellamy Partridge.

Staged by Ezra Stone.
Setting by Watson Barratt.

CAST

(In Order of Appearance)

FRIEDA	Norma Lehn
HERBERT GAGE	Robert Keith
SARAH GAGE	Lorna Lynn
PAULA GAGE	C. Nevil
MARGE GAGE	Lulu Mae Hubbard
BARBARA GAGE	Natalie Thompson
GEORGE HUSTED	John Hudson
JONATHAN ROCKWOOD	Charles Middleton
MATHILDA ROCKWOOD	Helen Carew
MR. LOOMIS	John McGovern
UNCLE WALTER	Charles Burrows
MATT ROCKWOOD	Irving Morrow
CARSON	Henry Jones

THE SCENE: *The living-room of an old house in Connecticut.
The Gage family, after restoring it to its Colonial state,
have just moved in.*

THE TIME: *The present.*

3

SYNOPSIS

ACT ONE, *Scene One: A morning in June.*
Scene Two: Evening of the same day.

ACT TWO, *Scene One: Next September (early morning).*
Scene Two: The following January (late afternoon).

ACT THREE: *Early the next morning.*

STAGE CHART

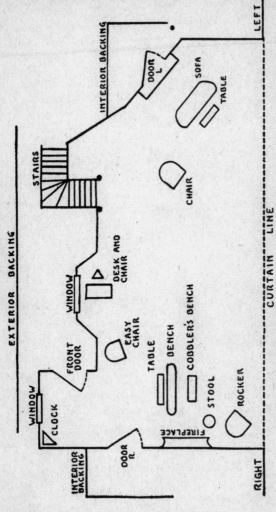

SUGGESTED SETTING FOR "JANUARY THAW." SEE "PROPERTY
PLOT" AT THE END OF THE PLAY FOR FURTHER DETAILS.

5

ACT ONE
Scene One

SCENE: *The house in Connecticut, where the Gage family lives, was built before the Revolutionary War. It, and especially the living-room in which this play takes place, has been enthusiastically restored to its Colonial state. Plaster, wallpaper, and paint no longer hide the living-room's fine old ceiling beams, its lovely old staircase, its wonderful old fireplace with its Dutch oven. The room has just been completed and its quaintness is a bit too bright—like an exhibition at Lord and Taylor's. Beneath the mantel hangs an ox yoke, and above the mantel hangs a sampler. One table lamp has been made out of a coffee grinder, and another out of a spice box. On window shelves on the back wall are old pieces of glass. The house's front door,* U R, *opens directly into the living-room. At* L *stage is the door of the master bedroom. In the rear,* U L C, *a staircase leads to the upstairs part of the house. There are windows on the first landing of the stairs. The door to the kitchen is* R. *(See stage chart on page 5 for further details.)*]

AT RISE OF CURTAIN: *It is a morning in June, last June.* HERBERT, *a nice enough looking man in his forties, is pacing back and forth, trying to get an idea for his new book. An idea strikes him. He sits down at his desk and starts typing.* FRIEDA, *the hired help, a solid but youngish woman, enters* R, *carrying three ashtrays. She places a clean ashtray on the table above the bench, tests the dust on the table with her*

7

finger, goes to the front door, slams it shut, and then places an ashtray on the desk, and on the table D L. HERBERT *is working at his desk, unaware of her.*]

FRIEDA [*putting an ashtray on the table above the bench*]
Well, Mr. Gage, you certainly got yourself a nice place here to write in. A nice, *quiet* place. [*She slams shut the front door.*] If you don't do good you certainly can't blame it on your working conditions. They're ideal! But you will do good—I know you will. Mr. Gage, I certainly wish you every success in the world on your new book. [*She crosses to behind* HERBERT, *who hasn't heard.*] I wish you every success in the world, Mr. Gage!

[HERBERT *still doesn't hear.* FRIEDA *shouts.*]

FRIEDA
Good luck, Mr. Gage!

HERBERT [*jumping, startled*]
What? What, Frieda?

FRIEDA
Good luck!

HERBERT [*shouting back*]
Thank you!

FRIEDA [*angrily*]
You're welcome!

[FRIEDA *stamps out* L. HERBERT *realizes what he has done, leaps to his feet, and calls.*]

HERBERT
Frieda, Frieda . . . I'm sorry, Frieda. I apologize.

[FRIEDA *enters* L, *carrying a silent butler.*]

HERBERT

I didn't know . . . I'm sorry.

FRIEDA [*still angry*]

That's all right. [*She empties the ashtray on the table* D L.]

HERBERT

You don't have too much to do, do you? We eat the things you like, don't we? If we don't, speak up.

[FRIEDA *empties the ashtray on the desk.*]

HERBERT

You're more than a maid. You're one of the family, Frieda. [*He adds quickly.*] You're more than one of the family.

FRIEDA [*not taken in*]

Is that so? I never heard you yell at the rest of the family like that.

HERBERT

Why, you just haven't been listening. Frieda, just as soon as we can we're going to build a wing on this house. And you can live right here. Right in the bosom of the family. You won't have to ride the bus back and forth to work.

FRIEDA [*emptying the ashtray on the table* R, *coldly*]

I don't mind the bus so much.

HERBERT

Frieda, I don't think I told you . . . I'm going to dedicate this new book to you.

FRIEDA

    You are?

HERBERT

    Yes, sir! "To Frieda: whose sympathy and understanding have made this book possible."

FRIEDA [*pleased now*]

    Why, thanks . . . thanks a lot. You know, Mr. Gage, I could be working in town at the Kimberleys'. For much more money. [*She faces front.*] But I like you folks.

HERBERT

    Yes, Frieda, there are things in life more important than money.

FRIEDA [*smiling admiringly*]

    You express yourself so beautiful, Mr. Gage. Well . . . good luck on your book.

HERBERT

    Our book, Frieda. Thank you.

FRIEDA [*completely charmed, laughing*]

    Don't mention it, Mr. Gage . . . after all . . .

    [FRIEDA *goes out* R. HERBERT *heaves a great sigh of relief, and goes back to his typing. He makes a mistake, x's out the mistake, and starts typing again.* SARAH *runs down the stairs. She is twelve, going on thirteen, and large for her years.*]

SARAH [*coming down the stairs*]

    Hurry up, Paula.

PAULA [*offstage*]

    Okay!

SARAH
Oh, Daddy, you're working! Have you had your breakfast already?

HERBERT [*still typing*]
Hours ago, Baby.

SARAH [*tapping him on the back*]
Well, good luck on your new story.

HERBERT
Thank you, Sarah.

[HERBERT *and* SARAH *shake hands.*]

SARAH [*crossing to right of the desk*]
It's going to make the best-seller list! I know it is!

[PAULA *comes down the stairs. She is a year or so younger than* SARAH, *and pretty much of a tomboy.*]

PAULA
Good morning, Dad.

HERBERT
Hello, Paula.

PAULA [*tapping him on the back*]
Good luck on your new story.

HERBERT [*shaking hands with* PAULA]
Thank you, Paula. It's going to make the best-seller list.

PAULA
It better. Fixing up this old house cost a lot of money.

[MARGE *enters from* R. *More accurately, a churn filled with dogwood enters. When it is lowered down on the stool at*

D R *stage, there is* MARGE. *She is in her early forties, vivid and quick. She crosses* D R *and puts the churn on the stool.*]

MARGE

Oh! So sorry to be late, darling! I wanted the room to be perfect for you. [*She steps back and looks at the churn.*] Please admire it, Herbert. I spent days sandpapering that churn.

HERBERT [*crossing down, kidding her*]
But it was worth it! You've brought out the character in that churn!

MARGE
Paula, help me.

PAULA [*crossing down from the desk*]
Okay.

[MARGE *and* PAULA *carry the churn to the platform* U R.]

SARAH [*crossing to* HERBERT]
What if we need a churn for a churn some day?

HERBERT
Don't worry. Your mother will sandpaper one out of an old cellar door.

[SARAH *crosses to the sofa, sits, and eats peanuts and reads.* PAULA *crosses above the table* R, *and stands reading a detective magazine.*]

MARGE [*crossing down and putting her hat and garden gloves on the table* R]
We'll never know how lucky we were to find all these gorgeous old things in this house.

HERBERT [*glancing about the room*]

The boys at the antique shop can turn anything into a lamp.

MARGE

Can't they, though? [*She turns the handle of the coffee grinder lamp on the table* R.] Just think, probably generations and generations of coffee had been ground in that. [*She examines the room.*] Well, if I may say so, there isn't a nicer room in the State of Connecticut. It's perfect now. [*She looks at the chair right of the sofa, and crosses to it.*] Except maybe for that chair . . .

HERBERT

It's fine—now, let it alone.

MARGE [*crossing* L *and surveying it*]

I don't know. I like it when it's empty, but the moment somebody sits in it . . . [*She shakes her head.*]

HERBERT

Put a sign on it: "Wet Paint!"

[PAULA *crosses down left of the table* R *and sits on the stool.*]

HERBERT

You know, we certainly picked a fine time to remodel a broken-down, falling-down, two-hundred-year-old house. The material shortages, the prices so high. [*He shrugs.*] But what the heck!

SARAH [*who is lying on the sofa reading, looking over her shoulder*]

Exactly! What the heck!

MARGE

You know, from the very first moment I saw this old house I fell in love with it. That sort of thing has only happened to me twice in my life. [*She laughs, and crosses up to behind* HERBERT.] You didn't look much better than this house, Herbert.

[PAULA *lies down on the floor at* C *stage and reads the detective magazine.*]

MARGE

Well, you look fine now. Both of you do.

HERBERT

Thanks!

MARGE [*crossing to right of the desk, excitedly*]

I forgot to tell you. One of your radishes is up—this high! [*She indicates.*]

HERBERT [*pleased*]

Really?

MARGE [*sitting in the chair right of the desk*]

I'm so proud of you, darling. Oh, Herbert, it's going to be wonderful! Hundreds and hundreds of jars of peas and beans and tomatoes and corn, and everything! No more telephoning the grocer every time I need something.

SARAH

If we had a telephone.

MARGE [*excitedly*]

Oh, darling, that reminds me! The Gleasons cancelled their order for a telephone. Now we're only forty-ninth on the list.

HERBERT

If I don't make some money with this new book we'll have to ask for our deposit back.

MARGE

Yes! [*She rises and turns to the children.*] You two—run, scat! At last we've got you out of a stuffy New York apartment and into the country. Now, please get some good out of it!

SARAH [*rising and crossing* R, *to* MARGE]

Darn it, Mother!

[PAULA *rises and crosses to right of the bench, throwing the magazine on the cobbler's bench in passing.*]

MARGE

Sarah!

SARAH [*crossing to right of* MARGE]

Why can't I have a horse right away? What's the use of living in the country if you can't have a horse?

MARGE

Some day we'll have a horse.

SARAH

A horse would pay for itself in no time.

MARGE

What?

SARAH

Sure. Daddy wouldn't have to spend so much money on fertilizer.

[MARGE *pushes* SARAH *toward the kitchen door,* R. SARAH *goes out* R, *and* PAULA *follows, shaking her head.*]

MARGE

There, Herbert. [*She crosses to the stairs.*] Well, good luck, darling! [*She turns and pauses.*] Herbert, I've had the most disturbing dreams lately about the Rockwoods . . . old Mr. and Mrs. Rockwood. I dreamed they weren't dead. That they were coming back here. Oh, but that's not possible! They couldn't be anything else but dead after all these years. Dreams are silly, aren't they, Herbert?

[HERBERT *is working, oblivious to her.* MARGE *eases toward him.*]

MARGE

Darling, you aren't hearing a word I say!

HERBERT

Yes, I am. Do anything you want to it, Marge. Paint it green, if you want to.

[MARGE *laughs, shrugs, and goes up the stairs to change her dress.* HERBERT *goes back to work. He has a little more trouble this time. He types. Then he rises, moves* D L, *picks up the ashtray, now filled with peanut shells, looks about for the wastebasket, and then dumps the peanut shells in the spice box. He sits, spits on his hands, and starts typing furiously.* BARBARA *enters from the stairs. She is twenty-one, attractive, and warm.*]

BARBARA

Good morning, Father.

HERBERT

Oh, hello, there.

[BARBARA *kisses him*.]

HERBERT

Where's your man, George?

BARBARA [*looking upstairs*]

He'll be down soon. I heard him in the shower.

HERBERT

How does he sound in the shower? That's important.

BARBARA

Dad, stop it! [*She crosses right of the desk, turns back, and sits on the upstage arm of the chair right of the desk.*] Listen, Dad, unless my woman's intuition is off the beam, George has that look in his eye. I think he's going to ask you if he can marry me. Will you help him out?

HERBERT

You bet. [*He goes back to work.*]

BARBARA

George isn't much of a salesman, Dad. He'll need a lot of co-operation from you. Or else he'll end up by just asking you what time it is. He's very reticent. So if you'll just——

[HERBERT *is drumming impatiently on the desk.*]

BARBARA

Oh, I'm sorry, Dad. You're trying to work. We'll talk about it later. I'm going down the lane for the mail. [*As she goes out and leaves the door open she calls:*] Good luck—Mr. Genius.

[BARBARA *goes out the front door.* HERBERT *types, x's out a mistake, and goes back to his typing.* GEORGE HUSTED *enters from the stairs. He is a rangy young man of twenty-one.*]

GEORGE [*on the bottom step*]

Good morning, Mr. Gage.

HERBERT [*continuing typing*]

Good morning, George.

GEORGE [*standing there uncertainly*]

Mr. Gage, I hate to interrupt you. But I'm getting out of college soon.

HERBERT

Fine! Everybody should!

GEORGE

I'm going back to California this evening, you know, and . . .

HERBERT

I don't blame you.

GEORGE [*crossing to him*]

Look, Mr. Gage . . .

HERBERT

Yes? [*He stops typing.*]

GEORGE

I love your daughter and . . . I love your daughter and . . .

HERBERT

You love my daughter and you have every reason to believe my daughter loves you.

GEORGE

Well . . . I don't know . . . [*He turns downstage.*]

HERBERT

Confidentially, George, she is definitely that way about you. [*He starts typing again.*]

GEORGE

Gee, thanks!

HERBERT

Why don't you two get married?

GEORGE [*crossing up to* HERBERT]

That's exactly what I wanted to talk to you about!

HERBERT

Oh!

GEORGE [*laughing*]

C'mon, cut it out. [*He speaks seriously.*] I haven't said anything to Barbara yet. I mean, not anything definite. I wanted your advice first.

HERBERT

Sit down, George. [*He starts typing.*]

GEORGE

Thanks.

[HERBERT *rises as* GEORGE *crosses down and starts to sit in the chair right of the sofa.*]

HERBERT

Oh! Oh! Not there! That chair looks better empty!

[GEORGE *jumps out of the chair before he has completely sat down.*]

GEORGE [*crossing to* R C]

It's like this. I might get out of college in two months or maybe not till the end of the term. It's all a mix-up about my credits. [*He turns* L.] But whenever it is, the first thing I want to do is marry Barbara. Would that be a mistake?

HERBERT

A mistake **for you** or a mistake for Barbara?

GEORGE

I have some money saved but I don't have a job. I know I can get a job, but—well, I don't want you to think I'm irresponsible. I understand about the rent coming due.

HERBERT

Oh, you don't have to worry about the rent. The housing shortage takes care of that. We have a house here, and if worst comes to worst I could always quit writing and go to work. [*He crosses up to the desk and sits.*]

GEORGE

I wouldn't want you to do that. [*He pauses.*] I've got her on my mind all the time.

HERBERT [*starting to type*]

Why don't you marry the girl? Then you can forget about her. She's outside. Go ask her.

GEORGE

Supposing she says "no"?

HERBERT
Five bucks says she doesn't.

GEORGE [*facing front*]
Well, she might say "yes" just because she's sorry for me.

HERBERT [*exasperated*]
Will you get out of here! I've got work to do.

GEORGE [*crossing up to the front door*]
I'm sorry, I——Thanks a lot. [*He takes a deep breath.*]
Well, here I go! [*He turns and crosses down to the back of
the chair right of the desk.*] Just one more thing.

HERBERT [*stops typing, wearily*]
Yes, George.

GEORGE
What did you say to Mrs. Gage when you asked her?

HERBERT
"Will you marry me?"

GEORGE
"Will you marry me?" That sounds okay. "Will you marry
me?"

HERBERT
Barbara.

GEORGE
Barbara. Thanks! You're a pal!

[GEORGE *goes out and shuts the front door.* HERBERT *shouts
after him.*]

HERBERT

Hey, George!

[GEORGE *apparently stops.*]

HERBERT

Good luck!

[HERBERT *goes back to his typing. Then in the distance can be heard the wailing of a country fire siren. After a moment,* SARAH *dives in from the kitchen,* R.]

SARAH [*offstage*]

Fire! Fire! [*She enters* R *and crosses to* L *stage, to the wall pegs, for a sweater.*] Fire, Daddy! Fire! Fire!

HERBERT [*rising and crossing* R]

What a time to have a fire! [*He takes his slippers off.*]

[PAULA *runs in* R.]

PAULA

There's a fire, Daddy!

[PAULA *rushes to the wall pegs for* HERBERT'S *hat.* SARAH *returns from the pegs with an old slipover sweater emblazoned with a college varsity letter. She holds it up.* HERBERT *dives into it.* PAULA *is ready with the hat. She slaps it on* HERBERT'S *head, and then starts for the kitchen door.*]

PAULA

Your hat!

[FRIEDA *hurries in* R *with a leather jacket, and holds it for* HERBERT, *who slips into it.*]

FRIEDA

Here's your jacket, Mr. Gage!

PAULA

I'll get the gate open!

[PAULA *is out the kitchen door,* R. MARGE *is coming down the stairs.*]

MARGE

The car keys, Herbert—the car keys!

[HERBERT *holds them up for her.* MARGE *takes them and rushes by, to the kitchen door,* R.]

MARGE

Oh, I hope it starts!

[MARGE *dashes out* R.]

HERBERT

Now, I've got everything! [*He starts for the kitchen.*]

FRIEDA [*yelling*]

Your boots, Mr. Gage!

SARAH [*crossing* L]

That's Barbara's job! Where is she?

[SARAH *goes out* L.]

FRIEDA

I'll hold the kitchen door open for you!

[FRIEDA *picks up his slippers and goes out* R. SARAH *is back in* L *with the boots, leaving the door to the bedroom open.* HERBERT *goes to sit in the chair right of the sofa, realizes that's the good chair, and sits on the sofa.*]

SARAH

Can't I go with you this time?

HERBERT [*fussing with his boots*]

No!

SARAH

Aw!

HERBERT

You know you can't!

SARAH

Oh, well, anyway, Daddy, I'm proud of you. A fireman!

HERBERT

Just a volunteer. Just two more fires and I'll be off those
damn pumps—and then I'll rate a helmet.

[*There is a knock at the front door.*]

HERBERT

Come in, come in!

[JONATHAN ROCKWOOD *steps in, followed by his wife,*
MATHILDA. JONATHAN *is an elderly man, but he is tall, still
spry, and full of ginger. His wife is small, not so lean as
he, not so weatherbeaten, but sturdy. They are a pair of
Connecticut Yankees.* MATHILDA *is nervous, but not* JONA-
THAN.]

HERBERT

Good morning! Come in and sit down. Sit down and make
yourselves at home. Sarah, tell your mother—company. [*He
turns to the* ROCKWOODS.] Pardon me, I've got to put out
a fire!

[HERBERT *runs out* R.]

SARAH [*closing the door*]
Be careful, Daddy.

[HERBERT *is gone.* SARAH *turns to the visitors.*]

SARAH
Good morning.

MATHILDA
How-do-you-do?

JONATHAN
Howdy.

[SUSAN *looks past them, out the front door, and sees something that makes her forget all about the fire.*]

SARAH
Oh! [*She crosses to left of* JONATHAN *and* MATHILDA.] Is that your horse out there? Hitched to the wagon?

JONATHAN
Yep.

SARAH
He's a beautiful horse, beautiful. [*She turns to* JONATHAN.] What's his name?

JONATHAN
Name's Shadrach.

SARAH
Can I pat him?

JONATHAN

Guess so. But don't tell him he's beautiful. Got enough trouble with him as it is.

SARAH

Oh, thank you! [*She starts out the front door.*]

JONATHAN [*taking her by the hand*]

What's your name, little girl?

SARAH

Sarah.

JONATHAN

Sarah what?

SARAH

Sarah Gage. G-a-g-e. Gage.

MATHILDA

That's the name on the mailbox, Jonathan.

JONATHAN

Just makin' sure. [*He turns back to* SARAH.] Sarah, you won't forget to tell your mother that——

SARAH

Oh, no, I'll tell her you're here!

[SARAH *goes out the front door.* MATHILDA *and* JONATHAN *cross down.*]

MATHILDA [*nervously*]

Jonathan, what are we goin' to do? What are we goin' to do?

JONATHAN

We're goin' to let things happen in their own natural way.
Don't believe in forcin' things. So don't you start frettin',
Mathilda. We're in. And we was invited in. We're home.
Set down and make yourself comfortable. [*He speaks iron-
ically.*] Mr. Gage just said to.

MATHILDA [*sitting on the bench*]

Fine thing! Bein' asked to set down in your own house.

[JONATHAN *is looking upstage.*]

MATHILDA

Take your hat off, Jonathan.

JONATHAN

What for?

MATHILDA

We're goin' to pray.

JONATHAN

Oh.

[JONATHAN *crosses* R *and sits on the bench, holding his
hat and satchel on his lap.*]

MATHILDA

Our Heavenly Father, we thank You for bringin' us back to
Connecticut and to our house. We thank You for watchin'
over us these six years we have been gone—for carin' for us
in Montana and Wyoming and Idaho and Oregon and——

JONATHAN

He knows where we been.

MATHILDA
  I'm bein' grateful to Him, Jonathan.

JONATHAN
  He knows it.

MATHILDA [*ignoring him*]
  And we ask You not to let our son Matt get in no more
  trouble, so we don't have to ever leave Connecticut and
  home again.

JONATHAN [*starting to rise*]
  Amen.

MATHILDA [*pulling him back by the wrist*]
  But we thank You for givin' Jonathan the chance to travel
  all through the West and see how they do their farmin' out
  there and to work on some of them farms and for curin' me
  of my long sick spell in Indiana and for keepin' Matt a good
  boy all the while since we got him out of trouble the last
  time. . . .

  [JONATHAN'S *attention has been wandering.*]

MATHILDA [*to* JONATHAN]
  You think it was wise to let Matt come on from Pittsburgh
  in the train?

  [JONATHAN *is looking off* L.]

MATHILDA
  Jonathan!

JONATHAN
  Oh! Didn't know whether you was talkin' to me or the Lord!

MATHILDA

Talkin' to you!

JONATHAN

Had to let him come on ahead. Had to lighten the load on
account of Shadrach.

MATHILDA

Well, I'll feel easier when I know he's at Uncle Walter's,
waitin' for us.

JONATHAN

Promised, didn't he?

MATHILDA

We could drive down to Uncle Walter's and see.

JONATHAN

Shadrach's done in. Word'll get around we're home, and
Uncle Walter'll bring Matt to us.

MATHILDA

I worry 'bout Matt.

JONATHAN

He'll settle down, now we're *home*.

MATHILDA

He was *home* when he run away from home.

JONATHAN

Stop frettin'. You through prayin'?

MATHILDA

Yes. Amen.

JONATHAN

Amen! [*He rises, puts on his hat, and crosses to* L *stage.*]
Wouldn't know the place was ours—except for the fireplace.
[*He has turned to face* R.] Sufferin' blazes—look at that!
[*He points to the ox yoke above the fireplace.*]

MATHILDA

Why, it's your old ox yoke.

JONATHAN

Hung in the barn forty years—ain't used that yoke since I
showed oxen at the Danbury Fair. What's it doin' there?

[MATHILDA *crosses up to above the table* R.]

MATHILDA

Jonathan! [*She goes to the lamp on the table.*] Know what
this is? My coffee grinder! [*She pulls open the drawer of
the coffee grinder and pulls out some cigarettes.*] Cigarettes!

JONATHAN

And look at that! [*He points to the lamp on the desk.*]

MATHILDA

My spice box! There ain't a lamp in the room that's made
out of a lamp!

FRIEDA [*offstage*]

Don't bother with those curtains, Mrs. Gage. I'll do them.

MATHILDA [*warningly*]

Jonathan!

[MARGE *enters* R, *quickly, brightly, the lady of the house.*]

MARGE [*crossing toward* MATHILDA]
Good morning! So nice of you to drop in! I'm Mrs. Gage!

JONATHAN
And I'm Jonathan Rockwood.

MARGE [*breezing along*]
Please sit——[*Suddenly, she realizes who they are.*] Rockwoods! You can't be the Rockwoods that lived here. They're
dead!

JONATHAN
Dead? That so? [*He turns to* MATHILDA.] Hear that, Mathilda? We're dead.

MATHILDA [*nervously*]
Jonathan, don't tempt fate.

JONATHAN [*crossing* U L]
Mrs. Gage, we used to own this place and we still got a
right to live here. [*He slaps his hat on a peg and crosses to
above the sofa and rests his satchel on the back of the sofa.*]
When the Power Company wanted this property for the
water rights, I sold it to 'em on one condition. That me and
my family could stay here the rest of our days. No matter
whether they rented it, sold it, or gave it away. We still got
a right to live here. I've got the original papers right here
in my satchel.

MARGE [*crossing to a position between* JONATHAN *and* MA-
THILDA]
Mr. Rockwood, you can't live here! We live here. We
bought this house.

JONATHAN [*looking into the bedroom,* L]

Mathilda, I see your spinet piano is still in our bedroom.

MATHILDA [*easing over* L.]

No!

MARGE

Your bedroom! That's ours. Herbert's and mine.

MATHILDA [*crossing to between* MARGE *and* JONATHAN]

My spinet piano! [*She turns to* MARGE.] Does it still play?

MARGE [*crossing to* MATHILDA]

We can't make it play—Mrs. Rockwood. Don't you understand?

MATHILDA [*crossing to the door* L]

Been a long time since I played my piano. [*She looks into the bedroom.*] Why, there's my *spool* bed.

MARGE

Yes, we found it here and——

JONATHAN

Mathilda, maybe you better lie down a spell and rest yourself.

MATHILDA

Soon as I unpack, Jonathan.

[MATHILDA *goes out* L.]

MARGE

Mrs. Rockwood, I don't think you should do anything until we all have a talk with my lawyer.

A scene from the last act of
"January Thaw."

JONATHAN

Ain't nothin' a lawyer can do. Mathilda and me got a right to live here until the day we die. And that might be quite a spell. My father reached the age of ninety-seven—[*He speaks ominously.*]—without even tryin'.

[JONATHAN *goes out* L. MARGE *covers her eyes with her hands.*]

CURTAIN

ACT ONE
Scene Two

AT RISE OF CURTAIN: *It is evening of the same day.* FRIEDA *is knocking on the bedroom door,* L. *It is opened slightly.*]

FRIEDA

If you've finished with your dinner I'd like to wash the dishes now.

[JONATHAN *appears* L *with a tray. He hands it to* FRIEDA.]

FRIEDA

Did you get enough to eat?

JONATHAN

More'n enough.

FRIEDA [*waiting in vain for the compliment*]

Well—was it good?

JONATHAN

You done your best, no doubt. Don't see any reason to hurt your feelin's.

[JONATHAN *goes out* L, *closing the door.*]

FRIEDA [*becoming angry, crossing* R]

Why, the nerve! The nerve—of all the nerve!

[FRIEDA *stamps toward the kitchen.* MARGE *hurries down the stairs and crosses toward the front door.* FRIEDA *turns back.*]

FRIEDA

Mrs. Gage! I want to talk to you!

MARGE

Not just now, Frieda. Mr. Loomis—my lawyer—is outside. [*She opens the front door.*] He just drove up. [*She calls through the screens.*] Hello, Mr. Loomis!

[FRIEDA *goes out* R. MR. LOOMIS *enters at the front door. He is a brisk, middle-aged man, and very businesslike. He carries a fine brief case.*]

LOOMIS

Good evening, Mrs. Gage.

MARGE

Thank Heavens, you're here!

LOOMIS

Sorry that I was tied up this afternoon. Well, they're back, are they?

MARGE

They arrived this morning.

LOOMIS

I warned you of that possibility. Mr. Gage here?

MARGE

No—he's putting out a fire. He left before the Rockwoods came. Mr. Loomis, I can't tell you how relieved I am to see you. If the Rockwoods were still here when Herbert gets home—well, he'd be terribly upset.

LOOMIS

I don't know what can be done but I'll try. Let me talk to Rockwood. [*He sits in the chair right of the desk, leaving his brief case on the desk.*]

MARGE [*crossing* L]

I told them it was silly to unpack their things, but . . .
[*She pauses.*] Well, Frieda and I will help them pack again.
[*She knocks on the door* L.] Mr. Rockwood.

[MARGE *starts to knock again.* JONATHAN *opens the door.*
MARGE *steps back, flustered.*]

MARGE

Mr. Rockwood—uh—I've got somebody here I want you to
meet. [*She smiles a gracious, social smile and crosses to*
LOOMIS.] Mr. Rockwood, this is my lawyer.

[LOOMIS *rises and crosses down.*]

JONATHAN

Your lawyer, eh?

MARGE

Yes, Mr. Loomis.

JONATHAN [*a toothpick in his mouth, crossing a few steps toward them*]

Loomis—you old Morton Loomis' son?

LOOMIS

Grandson. [*He is pleased.*] You knew my grandfather, did
you?

JONATHAN

Yep, I did. And old Mort'd turn over in his grave if he
knew any kin of his was a lawyer.

LOOMIS [*stiffly*]

It was my grandfather's money that put me through law
school.

JONATHAN

You must've stole it from him.

[LOOMIS *crosses to* JONATHAN. MARGE *eases over toward* R *stage.*]

LOOMIS [*clearing his throat, irritated*]

Mr. Rockwood. We're faced here by a rather peculiar situation. When you abandoned this place six years ago——

JONATHAN

Hold on there. We took a little trip, that's all. Stayed away longer than we expected. Why, we left all our household goods and furniture right here—and they're still here. . . . [*He surveys the room, taking in the chamber pot, and the lamps.*] Disguised in one way or another.

[MARGE *crosses up to left of the desk.*]

LOOMIS

Well, the question of abandonment is an issue to be decided by the court.

JONATHAN

The court won't have no trouble decidin' that. If we'd abandoned the place we wouldn't be here now.

LOOMIS

I'm not sure you are here. . . . In a legal sense.

JONATHAN [*snorting*]

Shyster lawyer talk!

LOOMIS [*really irritated, turning R, and then back to* JONATHAN]

Now, Mr. Rockwood, my client——

[MARGE *eases downstage.*]

JONATHAN

Don't know what you're goin' to say, but whatever it is it'll make old Mort turn over in his grave.

LOOMIS [*controlling himself*]

My clients might be persuaded to pay you a reasonable sum for your claim on this house.

JONATHAN

Knew it! Bribery! There goes old Mort! [*He makes a circular gesture toward* R *with his hand.*]

LOOMIS

Bribery nothing! It's a legitimate offer.

JONATHAN

Loomis, if Mathilda and me didn't live here, where *would* we live? There ain't no place.

LOOMIS

I appreciate that fact, Rockwood, but——

JONATHAN

And besides, even if there was an empty house in Connecticut, I wouldn't take it. There ain't no house for me and Mathilda 'cept this house. She was born in it. I married her in it.

[MARGE *eases toward* R *stage.*]

LOOMIS

All right! We've tried to settle amicably and you won't

co-operate. That's too bad. There's a way to get you out of this house, and I'll find it. I'm going to fight you, Rockwood.

[MARGE *turns back.*]

JONATHAN

I'll be right here, Loomis. Glad to fight with you any time. [*He crosses to the bedroom door, shaking his head.*] Certainly is surprisin' how far downhill a family can go in two generations.

[JONATHAN *goes out* L.]

MARGE [*crossing to* LOOMIS]

Mr. Loomis, you *can* get them out?

LOOMIS

Mrs. Gage, I went to Harvard Law School. [*He crosses up to right of the desk and gets his brief case.*]

MARGE [*crossing up to left of the desk*]

Oh—I'm glad. But, in the meantime, we have to let them live here?

LOOMIS

I'm afraid so.

MARGE

Oh, dear . . . [*She is standing left of the desk.*]

LOOMIS

This is a very difficult case, Mrs. Gage, but I'll do my best. [*He starts to cross to the front door.*] And now, good evening. I don't want to miss—[*He names a prominent news commentator.*]

[LOOMIS *goes out the front door, abruptly.* FRIEDA *enters* R, *immediately; she has been listening, of course.*]

FRIEDA

Now you can talk to me, Mrs. Gage.

MARGE [*sitting in the chair left of the desk*]
Oh—Frieda—yes, I suppose . . .

FRIEDA [*crossing to right of the desk*]
Mrs. Gage, I come to you with the understanding I was to work for one family and only one family.

MARGE

This is just temporary, Frieda—until Mr. Loomis——

FRIEDA [*going on*]
I cooked and give them lunch and dinner.

MARGE

We couldn't let them go hungry. . . .

FRIEDA

And not so much as "thank you"! In fact, that old buzzard slammed the door in my face.

MARGE

Frieda, please . . .

FRIEDA

Oh, I know this ain't your fault, Mrs. Gage, but after all!

MARGE [*rising, crossing to* FRIEDA]
Frieda, *I'll* do all that's necessary for Mr. and Mrs. Rockwood. You needn't lift a finger.

FRIEDA

Oh, no, thanks! I'd just as soon have that old buzzard's wife buzzin' around the kitchen as I would you.

MARGE

But I'd stay out of your way.

FRIEDA

No! And that's final! [*She crosses* R, *to the table.*] Besides, you got enough to do. And incidentally!

MARGE

Yes.

FRIEDA [*running a finger along the table*]

Look at that! When did you dust in here last? Dusting is your department, Mrs. Gage.

MARGE

Monday. Or maybe it was Saturday.

FRIEDA

Or maybe it was Friday. Mrs. Gage, a little less sandpapering, if you don't mind, and a little more dusting.

MARGE [*very contrite*]

I'm sorry, you won't have to speak to me again. [*Worried, she looks out the window* U C.] Can you still see smoke from the fire?

[BARBARA *and* GEORGE *enter at the front door.*]

FRIEDA

I ain't noticed.

BARBARA
  Is Dad back yet? Does he know?

MARGE
  No, he doesn't.

  [GEORGE *and* BARBARA *turn and look out the window* U R.]

GEORGE
  The fire must be out.

BARBARA
  Yes. I saw the Tuttle boys ride past.

  [HERBERT *enters* R, *unnoticed.*]

MARGE
  I hope nothing's happened to Herbert.

FRIEDA
  Don't worry, Mrs. Gage.

MARGE
  I just don't know how I'm going to tell him.

HERBERT
  Tell him what? [*He throws his cap and jacket on the table*
  R.]

MARGE [*coming down*]
  Herbert! Darling, are you all right?

HERBERT
  Of course I'm all right.

MARGE
  Was anything saved?

HERBERT [*crossing down to below the bench*]
  The cattle. Most of the machinery. [*He brightens.*] I saved
  a cow!

MARGE
  That's fine!

  [FRIEDA *picks up* HERBERT'S *cap and jacket.*]

HERBERT
  All by myself. Singlehanded. [*He sees* MARGE'S *attention
  wander to the bedroom.*] Don't you want me to tell you
  about it?

MARGE
  Herbert, there's something I have to tell you first.

HERBERT [*crossing below* MARGE *to the desk and putting his
  sweater on the chair left of the desk*]
  Of course, if you're more interested in your trivial household
  affairs than in my heroism—but I don't save a cow every
  afternoon.

MARGE [*sitting on the bench*]
  I know, dear. Tell us about it.

  [FRIEDA *crosses down to right of the bench.*]

HERBERT
  I was standing there and——[*He looks around.*] Where are
  the kids? [*He calls.*] Paula! Sarah! I want them to hear
  about this. I was standing there and suddenly——

  [PAULA *enters from the stairs and crosses* D L.]

HERBERT

Paula, I saved a cow!

PAULA

You did?

HERBERT

I was standing there, and I heard this moo——

[SARAH *enters* R.]

HERBERT

Sarah, I saved a cow!

SARAH [*crossing to left of the table* R, *to* MARGE]

You didn't tell him yet, did you?

HERBERT

Tell me what?

MARGE

Go on about the cow, first, Herbert.

HERBERT

It was a frightened, desperate, soul-chilling moo. [*He illustrates.*] Moo-oo-oo.

MARGE

And you knew it was a cow.

HERBERT

Yes, I knew immediately it was a cow. Listen, if you don't want to listen——

MARGE

But we do! What happened then, darling? Tell us!

ALL

Yes, yes, do!

[FRIEDA *tosses* HERBERT'S *jacket and cap on the bench, moves below the cobbler's bench, and stands with folded arms.* HERBERT *takes out a handkerchief and holds it over his face as he crosses* R, *to the fireplace, and straddles the stool en route.*]

HERBERT

I tied a wet handkerchief over my face—and I groped my way through the smoke——

MARGE [*warningly, as he straddles the stool*]

Oh, darling!

HERBERT

It was hotter than the devil—and finally I located my cow and I started out. [*He grabs* FRIEDA *by the arm and starts to lead her. He crosses up and sees* MARGE *is not listening.*] You're not listening!

MARGE

I am, Herbert. Yes, I am! I heard every word. [*She rises and crosses to* HERBERT.] Darling, give me your wet handkerchief? I'll hang it up to dry. [*She takes his handkerchief.*]

[FRIEDA *starts toward the kitchen door,* R.]

MARGE

Herbert, there's something I want to tell you.

FRIEDA [*turning back*]

You going to tell him now, Mrs. Gage?

HERBERT
  Tell me what? What's happened?

SARAH
  Mother wants to be the one to surprise you.

HERBERT
  Surprise me?

MARGE
  Oh, dear! [*She crosses to* C.]

  [HERBERT *looks them all over. They are all watching him.*]

HERBERT
  Oh, I see. This is going to knock me for a loop, huh? Nobody wants to miss seeing me get knocked for a loop. Will somebody please——

MARGE [*crossing up to* BARBARA, *putting a hand on her shoulder*]
  Children, Frieda, Barbara, I want to be alone with your father.

BARBARA
  But, Mother, you may need me.

MARGE [*hurrying them out to the kitchen*]
  You and George go out to the kitchen and make your father a sandwich.

HERBERT
  I don't want a sandwich.

MARGE [*to* BARBARA *and* GEORGE]
  Go out to the kitchen, anyway.

[BARBARA *and* GEORGE *go out* R, *followed by* FRIEDA.]

MARGE [*to the children*]

You kids go on up to bed.

[PAULA *and* SARAH *go up the stairs.* MARGE *and* HERBERT *are alone now. She takes his jacket and cap from the bench, crosses to left of the desk, and picks up his sweater from the chair.* HERBERT *starts to cross* L *and stops.* MARGE *crosses up to the pegs and hangs the clothes. She shakes out the handkerchief and hangs it, also, and then turns and looks at* HERBERT.]

HERBERT [*during* MARGE'S *cross*]

Well, what is it, Marge? Well, don't leave me dangling like this.

MARGE

Well, Herbert, they're not dead!

HERBERT [*controlling himself*]

Oh, thank Heaven. They're not dead. Were they badly injured?

MARGE

What, dear?

HERBERT

Who isn't dead?

MARGE

Mr. and Mrs. Rockwood.

HERBERT [*the name means nothing to him*]

Oh—Mr. and Mrs. Rockwood are not dead.

MARGE

Not at all! They're here! [*She points to the bedroom.*] In there!

HERBERT [*desperately*]

Who—are—Mr.—and—Mrs.—Rockwood?

MARGE [*crossing to* HERBERT]

Why, Herbert—you know!

[MARGE *and* HERBERT *both stand below the desk.*]

HERBERT

I *don't* know!

MARGE

I remember telling you all about them. It was in our apartment on Sixty-fifth Street.

HERBERT

I don't remember.

MARGE

I do! Distinctly. I explained it all to you. About the deed. That the Rockwoods had a right to stay here. In this house. As long as they lived.

HERBERT [*slowly*]

Stay here—in this house—as long as they live?

MARGE

Yes. When they sold the place to the Power Company they reserved that right.

HERBERT

Stay in our house as long as they live!

MARGE

But when I told you about it, you didn't seem to think it mattered.

HERBERT

You *didn't* tell me about it! This is the first time——

MARGE

Now, Herbert! I remember exactly when I told you! You were taking a *shower*.

HERBERT [*crossing down to above the chair right of the sofa*]
Marge! An important thing like that and you tell me when I'm taking a shower.

MARGE [*crossing down to right of* HERBERT]
Oh, darling, don't you see? You wouldn't have let me buy the house.

HERBERT

Darn right I wouldn't have!

MARGE

This was the only place left in Connecticut, Herbert. If I hadn't taken it, we wouldn't have got out of New York for years. Then, it was such a bargain, Herbert. And the quaint old things that went with it. [*She glances* R.]

[HERBERT *gives a meaningful glance at the bedroom.*]

HERBERT

Yeh! Marge, listen, you're positive? Those people have a right to stay for the rest of their lives?

MARGE [*nodding*]
It's in the deed, Herbert.

HERBERT [*looking toward the bedroom*]

How do they look? Healthy?

MARGE

They're both sound as nuts! Oh, darling, they're going to live to be ninety-seven—and longer, if they try!

HERBERT

This is gruesome. What gave you the idea they were dead?

MARGE

Well, nobody had heard a word about them for years. And another thing—I felt it in my bones.

HERBERT

I see. You felt it in your bones. Did your lawyer—feel it in his bones, too?

MARGE

Mr. Loomis has been here. He promised to straighten everything out.

HERBERT

When?

MARGE

As soon as possible. So you see, this is just for overnight—their being here. [*She smiles bravely, cheerfully.*] Herbert, until we get rid of them we may as well make the best of it. I'm sure they're a nice quiet old couple. We'll probably forget that they're around.

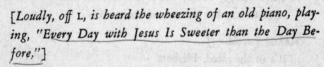

[*Loudly, off* L, *is heard the wheezing of an old piano, playing,* "Every Day with Jesus Is Sweeter than the Day Before."]

HERBERT

One of them plays the piano!

MARGE

Mrs. Rockwood.

[*The door* L *is opening.* JONATHAN *enters with a stagger-ing load of books. He slams the door after him and crosses* R, *toward the kitchen.*]

JONATHAN [*crossing between* MARGE *and* HERBERT]

Never seen so many books. That's what's wrong with this country—if people ain't readin' books they're writin' 'em.

MARGE

Oh, Mr. Rockwood—uh—this is my husband.

JONATHAN

Met him this mornin'! [*He stops at the door* R *and turns.*] What's that spaded section far side of the house?

HERBERT

My vegetable garden.

JONATHAN

That so?

[JONATHAN *chuckles and goes out* R, *into the kitchen, with the books.*]

HERBERT

What's he laughing about? What's funny?

MARGE

I have no idea. Darling, he said that he met you!

HERBERT [*his attention on the kitchen door*]

Yes, they got here just as I was leaving for the fire. But I didn't know who they were. What's he doing?

[JONATHAN *enters* R, *crosses* L, *to* L C.]

JONATHAN

I put them books in the kitchen.

HERBERT

Rockwood, I want to talk to you.

JONATHAN

Nothin' to talk about. What's right's right. Wastin' your money—hirin' a lawyer.

HERBERT

I wouldn't worry about our money, if I were you.

JONATHAN

Don't know what the country's comin' to. More lawyers in it than there are people. Somethin' the Democrats thought up.

HERBERT

What?

JONATHAN

Just like they thought up taxes and the high cost of livin'.

MARGE

The Democrats aren't in favor of a high cost of living!

JONATHAN

They're makin' it impossible to buy somethin' to eat. It's all a scheme. Democrats are tryin' to starve us Republicans to death.

MARGE

Prices are just as high for the Democrats as they are for the Republicans.

JONATHAN

See they got you fooled all right. [*He starts to cross* L.]

HERBERT

Rockwood, I don't want to discuss politics with you. What I want to say is this. I'll give you three days—no, I'll be reasonable. I'll give you a week to find another place to live.

JONATHAN

A week, eh?

HERBERT

Yes, and if you aren't out by then, I'll be forced to have you thrown out!

JONATHAN

Throw me out, eh? Gangster methods. Gage, mind if I ask you and your wife a question?

HERBERT

Of course not.

JONATHAN

Don't need to answer it if you don't want to. Wouldn't blame you for not admittin' it. You Democrats?

HERBERT

We voted Democrat the last four elections.

JONATHAN [*crossing to the bedroom door, pausing, turning, and then speaking*]

Thought so!

[JONATHAN *goes out* L.]

HERBERT [*turning to* MARGE]
Marge, did you tell them they could use our room?

MARGE
No! They just barged in.

HERBERT
Well, they've got to get out of there right now. Where are
we supposed to sleep?

[JONATHAN *and* MATILDA *come out from* L, *carrying an
early American cradle with a few sticks of firewood in it.
They plunk it on the floor.*]

MATHILDA
I don't expect Jonathan and me will be having a baby.

[MATHILDA *goes out* L *again.*]

JONATHAN [*scooping up the firewood*]
But these might come in handy.

HERBERT
Rockwood, I——

JONATHAN
Say, what d'ya call the color on the walls in there?

MARGE
Avalon buff.

JONATHAN
Enough to turn a man's stomach! What d'ya do with the
wallpaper that was in there?

MARGE
  We scraped it off! It took us days.

JONATHAN [*with a malicious twinkle*]
  Be obliged if you'd locate it and put it back on.

  [JONATHAN *goes out* L. *There is a knock at the front door.*]

MARGE
  Who is it?

HERBERT [*crossing to the front door, glancing out the window as he passes*]
  It's that old man from down the road. [*He opens the front door.*] Come in, come in.

  [UNCLE WALTER *enters at the front door. He is a shaggy little old man; he is Jonathan twenty years from now. He comes to the center of the room, inspects it minutely, and puts his hat on the table* R, *unhurriedly.*]

MARGE [*after a pause*]
  How-do-you-do?

UNCLE WALTER [*between* HERBERT *and* MARGE, *completing his inspection, then*]
  I'm eighty-six years old—mebbe eighty-eight. Been here, been there, been everywhere—Danbury, Bridgeport, even New York. Never seen anything like this. Where d'ye live?

HERBERT [*trying to laugh that off, then very loudly*]
  You're the man they call Uncle Walter, aren't you?

UNCLE WALTER [*turning to* HERBERT]
  Talkin' to me?

HERBERT

Why, yes . . . .

UNCLE WALTER [*wincing*]

I'm here. I ain't over in New York *State*.

HERBERT

Oh, sorry—I thought you were deaf—hard of hearing——

UNCLE WALTER

Never had a deaf day in my life. What made you think that?

HERBERT

Well, I've tried to speak to you several times—on the road—
and you never answered me.

UNCLE WALTER

Don't talk to people that move onto other people's property
unless I have to. Have to now. [*He turns to* MARGE.] Understand Jonathan and Mathilda are back?

MARGE

Yes.

UNCLE WALTER

I'll tell Matt. [*He starts for the front door.*]

MARGE

You'll tell who?

UNCLE WALTER

Matt. Jonathan's and Matilda's boy.

MARGE [*starting up*]

He's here! Here?

UNCLE WALTER

Outside. Waitin' in my buggy.

[*The bedroom door,* L, *flies open.* MATHILDA *rushes out.*]

MATHILDA

Matt! Mattie-boy!

[MATHILDA *is gone through the front door.* JONATHAN *appears, very pleased.* MARGE *turns upstage.*]

JONATHAN [*crossing to the front door*]

What d'ya know 'bout that! Mathilda looked out the window and there was Matt. [*He shakes hands with* UNCLE WALTER.] Howdy, Uncle Walter. Knew he'd keep his promise.

[JONATHAN *hurries out the front door.*]

UNCLE WALTER

Been two weeks since they seen that boy. You'd think it was two years.

HERBERT [*crossing to right of* MARGE]

I didn't know they had a son! [*He turns to* UNCLE WALTER.] Is he planning on staying here? In this house?

UNCLE WALTER

'Course.

HERBERT

But he can't!

UNCLE WALTER

Mathilda and Jonathan think the world and all of that boy.

HERBERT

Maybe they do, but——

UNCLE WALTER

Only boy they got.

HERBERT

Thank Heaven for that!

[MATHILDA *and* JONATHAN *enter at the front door, followed by* MATT. MATT *is surprisingly attractive in a quiet way. His mother, if she had ever gone to the movies, would*

*think that he looked like Gary Cooper. He is very neat—
almost dapper—and proper almost to the point of elegance.
His parents are chucking and fussing over him.]*

MATHILDA

It's been a long time. You come in, Matt.

JONATHAN

Come right in, Son, and set down.

[MATT *enters, suitcase in hand.*]

JONATHAN

This is your home much as ours. [*He shuts the front door.*]

[UNCLE WALTER *eases down by the fireplace.* MATT *sits in
the chair right of the desk.*]

MATHILDA

Here. [*She indicates the bench.*] You set down right here.

[MATT *rises, crosses down, and sits on the bench.* MATHILDA
is behind the bench, stroking MATT'S *shoulder.* JONATHAN
is also above the bench.]

MATHILDA

Uncle Walter, you took real good care of Matt, real good
care of him. Thank you ever so much.

[MARGE *and* HERBERT *listen intently, with chips on their
shoulders, waiting for an opening.*]

UNCLE WALTER

No trouble. Enjoyed it. Ain't had no steady company since
my Selma died.

MATHILDA

Matt, did you have a good trip on the train?

MATT

Train was awful crowded. Had to let a girl set on my lap at
Altoona, P-a. Asked her to get off at Harrisburg.

[MATHILDA *crosses down and sits left of him on the bench.*
MATT *slides over to make room.*]

MATHILDA

Well, we're home now! All of us. The whole family together!

JONATHAN [*crossing to left of the table* R]

Ain't never goin' to leave it again.

MATT

You shouldn't have left it in the first place. It was just plain
dumb. I wasn't chasing after that girl.

[HERBERT *eases toward* R *stage.*]

MATHILDA

'Course you weren't! The heathen! She was throwin' herself
at you. [*She shakes her head at him.*] Mattie-boy, Mattie-
boy, don't know where you got your good looks.

MATT [*modestly*]

Aw, Ma.

MATHILDA

Sometimes I wish you'd been born different. Guess you'll
be plagued by girls rest of your life.

HERBERT

Well, we all have some cross to bear! [*He crosses to left of*
MARGE.]

[MATHILDA *nods.* JONATHAN *glares.*]

MATT [*to* UNCLE WALTER, *rising*]

What ever happened to that Millicent Phillips?

MATHILDA

Don't want her name mentioned in this house! It was her caused all the talk.

MATT [*crossing and sitting on the stool*]

No. It was Gracie Cassala. [*He adds as an afterthought.*] And it wasn't really Gracie, but——[*He looks at* HERBERT *and* MARGE *over his shoulder.*] But let's not talk about that. [*He indicates them.*] That's Mr. Gage, isn't it? And Mrs. Gage.

MATHILDA [*nodding grimly and leaning toward* MATT]

They moved in while we was gone.

JONATHAN

Squatters. Democrat squatters. [*He crosses to right of the table.*]

MATT

Uncle Walter told me.

MATHILDA [*rising and indicating the bench*]

Set down, Uncle Walter. Visit with us a spell. Make yourself comfortable.

[HERBERT *crosses below* MARGE, *and* MARGE *eases R.* UNCLE WALTER *crosses to the bench.*]

HERBERT

It would be more convenient if you did your entertaining

some place else! [*He indicates the bedroom.*] You know, this is our *living-room*.

JONATHAN [*behind the bench*]

As much ours as yours. Set down, Mathilda. [*He starts to lead* UNCLE WALTER *to the rocker,* D R.] Set down, Uncle Walter.

MATHILDA

Uncle Walter better set there by the fireplace.

JONATHAN

Let him set where he wants to set.

MATHILDA

He's chewin' tobacco, ain't he? [*She turns to* UNCLE WALTER.] You're chewin', ain't you?

UNCLE WALTER

I'm awake, ain't I?

MATHILDA

Set by the fireplace.

UNCLE WALTER

This ain't one of my spittin' days. It's one of my swallowin' days.

MATHILDA

Sometimes you forget.

UNCLE WALTER [*counting alternate fingers*]

Monday, Wednesday, Friday are my swallowin' days. This is Monday, ain't it?

MATHILDA

It's Tuesday. [*She takes his arm.*] Set here.

UNCLE WALTER [*sitting on the bench*]

Didn't chew at Selma's funeral. And it got me all mixed up.

[JONATHAN *crosses down and sits in the rocker. The* THREE ROCKWOODS *and* UNCLE WALTER *make themselves at home around the fireplace.*]

MARGE

Herbert, do something! Don't——

HERBERT [*helplessly*]

What can I? I can't . . . [*He crosses* L, *to the sofa.*]

MARGE

This is impossible! [*She crosses* R.] Now, you listen. This is *our* living-room and we're going to use it! We're not leaving, we——[*Suddenly, she turns back to* HERBERT *and crosses* L.] Herbert, sit down, darling—sit down.

[MARGE *and* HERBERT *sit on the sofa. She smiles at him, a charming, social smile, and speaks loudly to him, conversationally as all getout, but too loud.*]

MARGE

Darling——

MATHILDA [*starting to talk at the same time*]

Well, how've——

[*They stop, and* MARGE *begins again.*]

MARGE

Darling, tell me—uh—what have you been doing with yourself all day—today?

HERBERT [co-operating, but not very well]

Oh, this, that, the other thing! [He laughs.] Uh—what have *you* been doing with yourself all day, today, darling?

[*The* FOUR VISITORS *have turned in their chairs and are listening, staring with amazed interest.* MARGE *laughs merrily, and* MATT *looks around at her.*]

MARGE

Oh, I've managed to keep busy!

[*There is a pause, and then* MARGE *and* MATHILDA *start to speak together again.*]

MARGE

Darling——

MATHILDA [at the same time]

Well, Uncle Walter——

[*The* TWO GROUPS *eye each other, and then:*]

MARGE

Darling! Has anything exciting happened to you today?

HERBERT

Some people dropped in.

MARGE

Oh! Anybody we know?

HERBERT

A man and his wife and—their little boy.

MARGE

Oh, how charming! Did they stay long?

HERBERT

No, not long—I hope. [*He laughs gaily. It turns sour.*]

[*There is a pause, and then:*]

MATHILDA

Well, how've you been, Uncle Walter?

UNCLE WALTER

Well, I'll tell you, don't chop kindlin' the way I used to twenty, thirty years ago.

JONATHAN

Don't, eh?

UNCLE WALTER

Nope. Chop it faster now.

[UNCLE WALTER *is pleased with himself. The* ROCKWOODS *laugh. There is a pause.* HERBERT *echoes with a horse laugh. There is another pause.* MARGE *suddenly starts to rise.* HERBERT, *a beaten man, pulls her down. He puts his hands over his eyes.*]

UNCLE WALTER

Mathilda, Jon, remember young Gorley?

MATHILDA

'Course I do. Matt stood up with him at his weddin'.

UNCLE WALTER

Broke his arm.

JONATHAN

That so?

UNCLE WALTER
Yep. Got it in a sling.

MATHILDA
How's his missus?

UNCLE WALTER
Same as usual. Expectin' a baby.

MATHILDA [*after the laugh*]
Can't beat them Gorleys.

[HERBERT *rises and crosses up toward the stairs.*]

UNCLE WALTER [*stirring in his chair*]
Well, time I was headin' down the road.

MATHILDA
Oh, no, Uncle Walter! Stay a minute. Been a long time since we talked.

UNCLE WALTER
You're right, Mathilda. [*There is a pause.*] Jon, see that those folks done away with your privy.

JONATHAN [*grimly*]
So I noticed.

UNCLE WALTER
Understand you got a new horse, Jon.

JONATHAN [*nodding*]
Old Jezebel died in Oregon.

UNCLE WALTER
Oregon—Oregon—that's up near Alaska, ain't it?

JONATHAN [*thinking a moment*]
Closer to Canada.

UNCLE WALTER [*nodding*]
Canada.

[*There is a pause.*]

JONATHAN
Didn't get into Canada.

UNCLE WALTER
Didn't?

JONATHAN
Nope.

[*There is a pause. The* ROCKWOOD *group is perfectly relaxed and having a wonderful time.*]

UNCLE WALTER
Didn't get into Canada, eh?

JONATHAN
Didn't, nope

UNCLE WALTER [*nodding*]
Didn't get into Canada.

HERBERT [*turning his head, moaning*]
Oh!

UNCLE WALTER [*slapping his knees and rising*]
Well, Jon, got to be goin'.

JONATHAN
'Night, Uncle Walter. [*He rises.*]

UNCLE WALTER

Enjoyed hearin' about your trip. [*He crosses up to the front door.*]

MATHILDA

'Night, Uncle Walter.

MATT

'Night, Uncle Walter.

UNCLE WALTER

Have to run over to the Simpsons' and tell them all about your trip. [*He turns at the door.*] Didn't get into Canada.

[UNCLE WALTER *opens the front door and goes out.* JONATHAN *crosses down and sits in the rocker.* HERBERT *crosses to the group at* R.]

HERBERT

Mr. Rockwood! Mrs. Rockwood! And—Master Rockwood!

MATHILDA [*shaking the dozing* MATT]

Wake up, Matt. Mr. Gage is goin' to make a speech.

HERBERT

Hardly a speech. I'm going to be brief and to the point.

[BARBARA *and* GEORGE *enter* R.]

BARBARA

Father, I'm sorry to interrupt, but George has to leave now. He's got to catch the nine-thirty. [*She sees* MATT *and turns to her father.*] Who's he?

[MARGE *rises.* MATT *rises and turns upstage.*]

HERBERT

Their son. Matt Rockwood.

MATT

How-do-you-do? [*He bows deeply from the waist.*]

BARBARA

How-do-you-do? [*She is disconcerted, and then takes* GEORGE'S *hand and introduces him.*] Mr. Husted—Mr. Rockwood.

MATT

Howdy.

GEORGE

How are you?

BARBARA

I'm going to drive George to the station now, Dad.

HERBERT

Okay. Be careful.

BARBARA

Oh, thanks!

GEORGE [*crossing to the stairs, quickly*]

I'll get my bag. We'll have to hurry.

[GEORGE *goes up the stairs.* HERBERT *sits in the chair left of the desk.* FRIEDA *enters* R *and crosses to* C. *She has on her hat and is carrying a black purse.*]

FRIEDA

Mrs. Gage, they can take me to the bus when they go to the station.

[BARBARA *has paused on the bottom step of the stairs.*]

MARGE

Yes, Frieda.

FRIEDA

I'll need some more money for the marketing tomorrow morning. [*She sees* MATT, *and she is very disconcerted.*] Why, Matt Rockwood! [*She crosses to* MARGE.] Is he going to stay here? Live here?

MATHILDA

'Course he is!

JONATHAN

'Course!

MARGE

Why, Frieda?

FRIEDA

I've heard all about him. I know that look. Excuse me!

[FRIEDA *runs back into the kitchen*, R.]

MARGE [*crossing* R]

Frieda.

[*But* FRIEDA *is gone.*]

MATHILDA

Now what got into her?

[MATT *sits in the chair right of the desk.*]

MATT

I don't know——never saw her before in my life.

JONATHAN [*rising, moving to left of the desk, to* HERBERT]
Crazy. Minute I seen her, I knew she was crazy.

MATHILDA

Must be crazy, poor thing. [*That takes care of* FRIEDA. *She rises.*] Jonathan, Mattie-boy, I've got a hankerin' for a nice cup of hot coffee before we go to bed. I've got some coffee beans and we can make a fire in the fireplace in our room and——[*She pulls the cord of the coffee grinder lamp out of its socket and starts to cross* L.]

MARGE [*stepping forward*]
Mrs. Rockwood! What are you doing?

MATHILDA

Got to grind my beans. Come along, Jonathan—Matt.

[MATHILDA *goes out* L, *followed by* JONATHAN. MATT *rises and starts to cross* L.]

HERBERT [*to* MATT]
Didn't get into Canada, eh?

[MATT *puts on his hat and goes out* L.]

MARGE [*crossing to* HERBERT]
Herbert, she took my lamp. Do something.

HERBERT

What? It's *her* coffee grinder!

MARGE

Oh, dear! . . .

[FRIEDA *enters* R. *She is carrying a net shopping bag containing her few clothes.*]

MARGE

Frieda, what on earth . . .

FRIEDA

Good-bye, Mrs. Gage. I enjoyed working for you. Good-bye, everybody. [*She crosses to* C.]

MARGE [*crossing to* FRIEDA]

You're quitting? Leaving? Why, Frieda?

FRIEDA

I won't stay in this house! Not with that Matt here!

[GEORGE *is coming down the stairs.*]

BARBARA [*easing downstage*]

Why? What is it about him that——

FRIEDA

He's got a reputation! That's what he's got, a reputation!

BARBARA

For what?

FRIEDA

For——Well, everybody in Ridgefield and Danbury knows! Believe me! There was one big sigh of relief when he went away. But now he's back!

GEORGE [*crossing to between the chair and sofa, left of* BAR-BARA, *and with his suitcase*]

C'mon, Frieda, tell us.

FRIEDA

Don't know if I can in mixed company, but . . . [*She hesitates, and then plunges ahead.*] Well, it's like this. George,

if I was you and I had a sister, and my sister was invited to
a picnic—and if Matt Rockwood was going to be at that
picnic, I'd pray for rain!

GEORGE

Hey, that guy's a wolf!

FRIEDA

I'm getting out of here! I'll wait for you in the car.

[FRIEDA *hurries out the front door.*]

MARGE

Oh, Frieda, you can't . . .

GEORGE [*crossing* R, *to* HERBERT]

Wait a minute! He's going to be living in this house with
Barbara here.

BARBARA

George, don't be silly! [*She comes downstage a step.*]

GEORGE [*crossing to* BARBARA, *throwing his suitcase on the
floor*]

Silly!

BARBARA

George, listen!

GEORGE

We're engaged! We're going to get married. Remember?

BARBARA [*kissing* GEORGE]

Darling! I can take care of myself! And besides, there's
Mother and Father——

SARAH [*unexpectedly, from the stairs*]

And there's *his* mother and father. Don't worry. She's safe! [*She folds her arms.*]

MARGE [*crossing below* HERBERT]

You get to bed, young lady. [*She crosses to* GEORGE.] George, now don't you worry. He's only going to be here for a week.

[SARAH *disappears from the head of the stairs.*]

HERBERT

I'll keep an eye on Master Rockwood. I'll keep both eyes on him.

GEORGE

I'd appreciate it, if you would, Mr. Gage.

BARBARA [*taking* GEORGE'S *bag and crossing* R]

Darling, you'll miss your train. Everything will be all right. C'mon, hurry!

GEORGE [*crossing* R, *below* MARGE *and* HERBERT]

Yeah—well, thanks, everybody. I had a swell time! [*He shakes hands with* HERBERT.] Mr. Gage, I'm depending on you!

HERBERT

I won't fail you, George.

BARBARA

C'mon, George!

GEORGE

So long, everybody.

[MARGE *crosses* R. GEORGE *and* BARBARA *go out the front door.* MARGE *and* HERBERT *are alone; everything is quiet. They stand looking at each other a moment. Then the bedroom door opens and* JONATHAN *enters* L. *He crosses to the desk and takes the spice-box lamp. He hands the shade to* HERBERT.]

JONATHAN

Mathilda wants her spice box. For spices.

[JONATHAN *goes out* L. HERBERT *crosses* L *with the shade, and drops it in the chair right of the sofa. He turns and looks at* MARGE. *She shakes her head at him.*]

MARGE

No, Herbert—let's not talk about it—now. [*She crosses* R.]

HERBERT

But where will you and I sleep, tonight?

MARGE

Oh, dear, let me see—Sarah can move in with Paula for tonight . . .

HERBERT

And I'll . . .

MARGE

And Barbara and I will share her room—and you, darling. You'll sleep there. [*She points to the sofa, and smiles.*]

HERBERT [*crossing to above the sofa, arranging the pillows*] Roomy, ain't it? [*He crosses to the window* U C *and closes the drapes.*]

[MATT *enters* L, *wrapped in a blanket.*]

MATT [*as he is coming through the door*]
  Good night, Paw!

  [HERBERT *turns just in time to see* MATT *lie down on the sofa
  and pull the blanket up under his chin.* MATHILDA *enters* L *in
  a dressing gown, takes the plant out of the chamber pot on
  the pedestal by the door, crosses down, and places the pot by
  the head of the sofa. Then she starts out* L.]

CURTAIN

ACT TWO
Scene One

AT RISE OF CURTAIN: *It is next September—early in the morning. The stage is quite dark. The living-room has changed. A dour picture of Calvin Coolidge hangs on the wall just left of the desk. If a large picture is not available, a small one in a frame may be placed on the desk. There is a new lamp on the desk, made out of a fine old kerosene lamp.* JONATHAN *enters* R *and crosses* L *with an armload of firewood. One piece falls as he reaches* L *stage. He picks it up and goes out* L. *We hear the logs being thrown down in the bedroom. The sleeping figure on a cot* D L *(made up as a bed) stirs in protest.* SARAH *is coming down the stairs. As she reaches the first landing she pulls the drapes open and lets in some light.*]

SARAH [*crossing above the sofa*]
Good morning, Uncle Jonathan!

[JONATHAN *appears at the door* L.]

JONATHAN
Mornin', Sarah.

SARAH
Have you fed and watered Shadrach yet?

JONATHAN [*shaking his head*]
Waitin' for you.

76

SARAH

Oh, thanks! [*She starts to cross* R.]

JONATHAN

Hold on, Sarah!

[SARAH *stops.*]

JONATHAN

Don't you get on Shadrach no more 'less I'm with the two of you.

SARAH

Aw . . .

JONATHAN

Shadrach's gettin' kinda skitterish. Now you mind what I say. I don't want your father suin' me. [*He crosses toward her.*]

SARAH [*by the desk*]

I promise! [*She sees the picture of Coolidge.*] I see you've got Calvin Coolidge up already!

JONATHAN

I do!

SARAH

Is he your hero, Uncle Jonathan?

JONATHAN

Never had a hero. But he was the best president we ever elected. [*He moves below* SARAH *to* R.] Kept his mouth shut and minded his own business.

SARAH

Aren't Mother and Father stubborn, though?

JONATHAN [*a tribute to the enemy*]

Pretty stubborn, all right. [*Then he continues, boasting.*]
But they ain't no more stubborn than I am. [*He crosses to
the front door and opens it.*] Fine mornin', Sarah.

SARAH [*following*]

Oh, yes!

JONATHAN [*as they go out the front door together*]
September's the best month God give us.

[*In a moment,* MARGE *enters* R *with a cup of coffee. She puts
the coffee on the desk, sees the Coolidge picture, and opens
the drapes,* U C. MARGE *takes down the Coolidge picture. If
it is a small one on the desk she turns it face down. Then
she goes to the foot of the cot and says* "Good morning,
dear." *She lifts the pillow, and* HERBERT'S *foot swings up.
She goes back to the desk, gets the coffee, and puts it on the
stool below the cot. She takes the pillow off* HERBERT'S *head,
says* "Good morning, dear," *and kisses him.* HERBERT'S *hand
gropes for the cup.* MARGE *hands it to him, and he drinks
with his sleep mask still on. She takes the mask off.*]

MARGE

Did you have a pleasant night, dear?

HERBERT

Huh?

[MARGE *removes* HERBERT'S *ear plugs.*]

MARGE

Did you have a pleasant night?

HERBERT

Of course not!

MARGE

Oh—did you have to count sheep again?

HERBERT [*bitterly*]

I don't count sheep any more. I count Rockwoods.

MARGE

Darling, please don't start the day by——[*She crosses to the desk and arranges things.*]

HERBERT

That son of theirs! Upstairs in a good bed—a room of his own! And me! I have to——

MARGE

You don't have to! Matt is perfectly willing to sleep down here.

HERBERT

He goes to bed at nine o'clock and the lights have to be out!

MARGE [*crossing down to above the foot of the cot*]

Well, Barbara could sleep in this room. That would make a place in Sarah's room. Paula could move out of my room into Sarah's—and then you could move into my room with me, where you belong.

HERBERT

How's that?

MARGE

Let's see—how did I——[*She speaks carefully.*] If Barbara moved down here, and——

HERBERT

You can stop right there! Barbara stays in a room with a door on it! As long as that Matt is in this house! I promised George.

MARGE [*getting his robe from the peg*]

But Matt's all right.

HERBERT

I don't trust him. [*He rises.*]

MARGE [*helping him into the robe*]

You know, either Matt's reputation is greatly exaggerated or else he's turned over a new leaf. Why, he doesn't even go out on Saturday night! Herbert, I really think he's settled down.

HERBERT [*sitting in the chair right of the desk*]

Settled down is right! He's settled down in this chair—like this. [*He rises.*] For weeks, for months, he has been sitting in this chair watching me, watching me. Could you write with somebody watching you—watching you?

MARGE [*crossing to the foot of the cot*]

Why in Heaven's name don't you ask him to sit somewhere else?

HERBERT [*kneeling on the cot, pulling a slipper out from under the downstage side*]

Because I'm not speaking to him.

MARGE

Herbert, you can't go on like this with the Rockwoods. Not speaking to them, hating them every minute. No wonder you can't write.

HERBERT

Let's not discuss it, shall we?

MARGE

I know it's unpleasant, having them here. [*She crosses* L, *below the cot, picks up the other slipper, and gives it to him.*] I don't like it, either. But what can we do about it? We can't leave here. We've got thousands of dollars tied up in this place.

HERBERT [*half-heartedly, getting into his slipper*]

Maybe we can sell it.

MARGE [*surprised at his suggestion*]

To whom? *Who* would buy it with the Rockwoods attached to it?

HERBERT

You're right. I can think of only one person. [*He looks at her.*]

MARGE [*handing the cup of coffee to* HERBERT]

And even if we could forget about the money, we couldn't go back to New York. There's no place to live there.

[HERBERT *sits on the bench.*]

HERBERT

Yeah, I know, I know. What's slowing Loomis up? Is he too busy to work on our case?

MARGE

He's working on it, constantly. He says it's rather compli-
cated and we mustn't expect a miracle. But, darling, the
point is—while they are here, it would be much pleasanter if
we learned to get along with them. We're intelligent, toler-
ant people. Or at least we were. Herbert, if we can't get
along with the Rockwoods, how on earth are we going to
get along with the Russians?

HERBERT [confused]

Huh?

MARGE

You know what I mean. [She takes a silent butler from the
cobbler's bench.] Herbert, there isn't a thing in the house
for lunch. Could Barbara drive me to town?

HERBERT

Look, why don't you do a whole week's marketing all at
once?

MARGE [crossing up to the desk and emptying the ashtrays]

I try to—honestly I do!

HERBERT

Well, there's always nothing to eat in this house.

MARGE

That isn't fair!

HERBERT

My mother always had something to eat in the house.

MARGE [stiffly]

Your mother had a telephone. She had an A & P right

around the corner. And she had only one child. And that is why he is so spoiled.

HERBERT

All right, I'm sorry. Why don't you get cases of things?

MARGE

You can't get cases of things nowadays. But I'll try. I promise I will.

SARAH [offstage]

Daddy! Mother!

[SARAH rushes in R and crosses to above the bench.]

SARAH

Come see Uncle Jonathan's beautiful——

HERBERT

Will you stop calling that man Uncle Jonathan! Damn it!

SARAH

Father, will you please refrain from swearing. Aunt Mathilda says that swearing shows people's ignorance.

HERBERT

Aunt Mathilda! You stay away from them!

SARAH

But, Daddy——

HERBERT

Did you hear me? Or do I have to put you over my knee?

MARGE

Herbert, don't. [She crosses to SARAH.] See Mr. Rockwood's beautiful what, Sarah? What has he?

SARAH

A cow! A man just brought it. He kept it for Uncle—[*She looks at* HERBERT.]—*Mr.* Rockwood, while he was out West. He would've brought it sooner, but it hasn't been at all well. Want to see it?

HERBERT [*sarcastically*]

And where is this beautiful sick cow of Mr. Rockwood's?

SARAH

He's milking it. Can you milk, Daddy?

HERBERT

Of course.

SARAH

Bet you can't.

HERBERT

It's simple. You sit beside the cow—down toward the tail. Reach under there, and there are four little faucets, and you squeeze them—milk! Of course it's harder to get cream.

[MARGE *laughs and crosses to the table* D L *and straightens the magazines.*]

HERBERT

Rockwood's no genius.

SARAH

Oh, yes, he is! Uncle Jonathan can do anything.

HERBERT

Marge, must they have a cow? They've got their son—[*He drinks his coffee on the laugh.*]—a horse, chickens, and now a cow. The next thing we know he'll have pigs!

SARAH [*crossing and sitting on the bench beside* HERBERT]
  Oh, haven't you seen his pigs?

HERBERT [*choking on the coffee, rising*]
  There! What did I tell you!

MARGE [*crossing up to the desk and straightening things*]
  You're right, Herbert.

HERBERT
  And have you seen their room lately? That wood sink in
  there. And that ancient cook stove!

MARGE
  I know! I know!

HERBERT
  And since daybreak he's been clumping through here and
  down the cellar with bushels of potatoes. In and out, up and
  down, down and up!

MARGE [*at the desk*]
  Herbert, we couldn't let them starve. We had to let them
  raise some food.

HERBERT
  But did he have to plant his garden right in the middle of
  my two-hundred-dollar lawn?

MARGE
  That's where you should have planted yours.

HERBERT
  What?

MARGE

Well, nothing grew in your garden!

HERBERT

What about my cucumbers? My cucumbers were terrific! [*He sits on the bench.*]

MARGE

Yes, they were—of course they were. And I'm very proud of my five pints of sweet-and-sour chow chow.

HERBERT

Three pints. Two pints blew up.

[JONATHAN *enters* R *with a milk pail and crosses* L.]

SARAH [*crossing* L, *to behind the sofa*]

Did she give a lot of milk, Uncle Jonathan?

JONATHAN

Yep. She done pretty good. [*He places the milk inside the door* L.] Mathilda will be tickled. Won't have enough milk to churn for a day or two, but it'll take that long to get this thing back in shape.

[JONATHAN *takes* MARGE'S *current floral display from the churn and throws it on the table* R. *He picks up the churn and starts for the bedroom.*]

HERBERT

Rockwood, I want to talk to you.

JONATHAN [*stopping at* L *stage*]

Guess I can spare a minute.

HERBERT [*crossing* L, *to the chair right of the sofa*]
  Rockwood, I understand you've got a cow.

JONATHAN
  That's right. Always had a cow. Always will have.

HERBERT
  Well, you can't keep it here. And that's final!

JONATHAN
  But I durned near didn't have a cow. Almost burned to
  death. Some feller pulled it out of the Lamberts' barn just
  in time.

  [HERBERT *groans and sinks into the chair right of the sofa.*]

JONATHAN
  Got to tend to my milk. Mathilda ain't up to it.

SARAH
  Is she sick, Uncle Jonathan?

JONATHAN
  It's her hip, Sarah.

SARAH
  Oh, I'm sorry.

JONATHAN
  Fell on them stairs there.

SARAH
  She did? Really?

HERBERT [*rising from the chair*]
  What's that? Your wife fell on those stairs?

JONATHAN [*nodding*]

They always was treacherous. With that red carpet on 'em they're even more so. [*He is going.*]

SARAH

May I watch you?

JONATHAN

C'mon.

[JONATHAN *and* SARAH *go out* L, *and the door is closed.*]

HERBERT [*excitedly, crossing to* MARGE]

Did you hear that, Marge—about his wife falling on those stairs, did you?

MARGE

Yes—I did.

HERBERT

Don't you see? He's going to sue us!

MARGE

Oh, Herbert! Do you think so?

HERBERT

Oh, I know his Yankee mind! Notice how casually he informed us about her hip—how easily. Then, bing! A lawsuit!

MARGE

Why, that would be dreadful!

HERBERT

This is one time he won't get the best of us. We'll nip his scheme right in the bud. What time is it?

MARGE

It isn't eight yet.

HERBERT

Good! You've just got time to catch Loomis before he gets to the office. Marge, you get in the car and do that while I get dressed.

MARGE [*crossing toward the door* R]

All right, Herbert, make your bed, so when Mr. Loomis——

HERBERT

Sure, sure!

[MARGE *goes out* R. HERBERT *goes back to the cot.* BARBARA *comes down the stairs, followed by* PAULA.]

BARBARA

Good morning, Dad.

PAULA

Hi, Dad!

HERBERT

Good morning.

BARBARA

Here, let me do that.

HERBERT

Thanks. Get that thing out of sight before Matt sees it!

[HERBERT *goes up the stairs.* BARBARA *and* PAULA *are fixing the cot.*]

PAULA

Where's Sarah?

BARBARA

She's in there with the Rockwoods.

PAULA [*crossing down to the foot of the cot*]

She's always in there. I've lost a lot of respect for Sarah—
selling her soul for a ride on a horse!

BARBARA

Oh, Paula!

[SARAH *enters* L, *carrying a pail. She crosses below* BAR-
BARA.]

BARBARA [*to* SARAH]

And what are you doing, my dear?

SARAH

Churning, my dear.

[SARAH *goes out* R. *An auto horn blows offstage.*]

BARBARA

There's the mail, Paula. Go get it.

PAULA

Okay!

[PAULA *goes out the front door.* BARBARA *pushes the cot
(the folding type) up to the stair well, and sees* MATT, *who
has entered down the stairs.*]

BARBARA

You! I thought you'd be on your way in to town to start
your job.

MATT [*crossing* R, *to below the desk*]

I decided not to take that job.

BARBARA [*pushing the sofa back in place*]

Oh, no! Why? You've got to do something. If you don't, Father will——

MATT

That job, behind the counter?

BARBARA

Wasn't it enough money?

MATT

It ain't the money—it's the principal of the thing. I'd be on my feet all day.

BARBARA

Matt, what kind of job do you want?

MATT

Oh, I'm not particular. [*He sits in the chair right of the desk.*] Anything, just so's it keeps me busy.

BARBARA [*pinning him down*]

What about the job in Danbury?

MATT

Couldn't get that job. They wanted my Social Security card. Ain't got none.

BARBARA

Didn't you ever have one?

MATT [*sitting forward*]

Nope. Social Security ain't good for a man. [*He sits back in the chair.*] Ruins his initiative. Besides, not so sure I could get one. Us Rockwoods don't look for no favors from Washington.

BARBARA [*exasperated*]

Matt, now you listen to me. Father's nearly a nervous wreck. And one of the reasons is you. Things are hectic enough without you sitting around in that chair all day. You've got to get a job, you've got to find something that will——

[BARBARA *sees* PAULA, *who enters at the front door with the mail.*]

BARBARA

Paula, any mail for me?

PAULA

Nope. I'm sorry. Not even from George.

[PAULA *puts the mail on the table* R *and goes out* R.]

BARBARA [*taking the mail off the table, crossing down, and opening a magazine*]

I haven't had a letter now for two days.

MATT [*rising and crossing toward her*]

That reminds me—you left your engagement ring up in the bathroom. [*He holds it out.*]

BARBARA

Oh, thanks! [*She puts on the ring, looks at it, sighs, and sits on the bench.*] It certainly is nerve-wracking for a girl not to know whether she's getting married next week, next month, or not till the end of the term.

MATT

I was afraid somebody would steal your ring.

BARBARA [*laughing*]

Matt! Who would steal it?

MATT

As many people as there are in this house—there might be one dishonest one among them.

BARBARA [*laughing at him, then seriously, kneeling on the bench*]

Matt, if only you fell in love. And got married. That's what you need—somebody to work for.

MATT [*crossing to L C*]

I don't know. I'd just like to see the look on your father's face, if I brought home a wife.

BARBARA [*impatiently*]

But you wouldn't. That's the point! You'd get a job. Buy a home of your own.

HERBERT [*from upstairs*]

Barbara! Who are you talking to?

[MATT *quickly goes out* L. BARBARA *sits on the bench.*]

BARBARA

Matt, Father.

[HERBERT *comes down the stairs. He crosses to* U R, *slipping a belt into his trousers.*]

HERBERT

I thought so!

BARBARA

Father—you're being silly about Matt. He——

HERBERT

I want you to stay away from him.

BARBARA

Oh, for goodness' sake!

HERBERT [*crossing up and opening the front door*]

You're always talking to him. What's so fascinating about him?

BARBARA [*laughing*]

I think he's kind of cute.

HERBERT

Cute! You and your mother! She doesn't see anything wrong with him, either!

BARBARA

There *isn't* anything wrong with him—except that he hasn't any ambition.

HERBERT [*crossing down to left of the bench*]

Oh, yes, he has. I've heard all about his ambitions. You stay away from him.

BARBARA

For Heaven's sakes!

HERBERT [*embarrassed*]

Barbara, has he ever—has he ever——

BARBARA

Asked for a date, or something? [*She laughs.*]

HERBERT

Has he? [*He crosses to right of the desk.*]

BARBARA

No—I guess I'm not his type. [*She rises and crosses to* HER-BERT.] Father, please, don't be silly about Matt. He lives here. He's somebody to talk to, that's all.

HERBERT [*looking out the window* U C]

Oh, here's your mother. With Loomis.

BARBARA

Loomis?

HERBERT

Business, just business. Baby, will you do something about breakfast? [*He is on his way to the front door.*]

BARBARA

Certainly.

[BARBARA *goes out* R. HERBERT *holds open the door and starts talking to* LOOMIS *before he enters.*]

HERBERT

Good morning, Loomis. Thank Heaven, Marge caught you in time!

[MARGE *and* LOOMIS *enter at the front door.* MARGE *closes the door.*]

HERBERT

Now, here's the situation——

LOOMIS [*crossing to the desk*]

I know the situation. Mrs. Gage explained it to me. No use going through it again. [*He looks at his watch.*] I've got to get to the office. Where's Rockwood? [*He sits in the chair right of the desk.*]

HERBERT

In there. [*He crosses* L *and stops.*] What's the procedure in a case like this? Do we have a doctor examine that hip?

LOOMIS

I'll handle this, Gage. If you'll just call Rockwood.

HERBERT

Yes, of course. [*He crosses to the door* L *and knocks, and then crosses back.*]

JONATHAN [*offstage*]

Yeah?

[JONATHAN *appears at the door* L.]

JONATHAN

Want to see me? [*He closes the door and leans on the down-stage door jamb.*] Hmm. See you got your lawyer.

LOOMIS [*rising and crossing* L]

Rockwood, I understand your wife fell on those stairs and hurt her hip.

JONATHAN [*warily, taking his time*]

Yep, she did. Caught her heel on the top step and down she come. All the way to the bottom.

LOOMIS

You've had a doctor, of course.

JONATHAN

Don't hold with doctors.

LOOMIS [*carefully*]

Well—under these—uh—peculiar circumstances, don't you

think you'd feel easier if your wife were examined by a first-class physician?

JONATHAN

Don't hold with physicians, either. [*He comes down and crosses to* L C.]

LOOMIS

Not if Mr. Gage is willing to pay the bill?

JONATHAN

Nope. Wouldn't be a party to anybody payin' good money to a doctor. Or a physician.

LOOMIS

But there must be something Mr. and Mrs. Gage could do.

JONATHAN

Hmm. [*He crosses down around the sofa and sits, throwing his hat on the sofa. Then he turns to* LOOMIS.] They want to do somethin'?

LOOMIS

Yes. I think they might be willing to.

JONATHAN

Well, now . . . [*He thinks a moment.*] They can take that tarnation pink carpet off them stairs.

[LOOMIS *sits in the chair right of the sofa.*]

MARGE [*crossing* L, *to* C]

That is not a "tarnation pink carpet"! It's a beautiful claret broadloom, and I won't have you——

JONATHAN

Better get it off there 'fore somebody else falls down them stairs.

MARGE

It's perfectly safe!

JONATHAN

Catches my heel every time I——

MARGE

That's ridiculous! That carpet——

HERBERT [*crossing* R, *to* MARGE]

Now, Marge, don't be unreasonable.

LOOMIS

Yes, Mrs. Gage. I think you'll be willing to remove it. On second thought. Won't you?

HERBERT

Yes, of course she will!

JONATHAN

I'm obliged to you, Mrs. Gage. [*Looking around the room, he points to the radio on the window ledge,* U C.] Then there's that infernal contraption there.

HERBERT

My radio!

JONATHAN

Never heard nothin' come out of it worth listenin' to.

HERBERT

Well, the nerve of you, with that God-awful piano you've got in there!

LOOMIS

Now, now, Gage——

HERBERT

But the news! How will I ever know what's happening?

JONATHAN

Uncle Walter will tell you.

HERBERT

What?

JONATHAN

Anythin' important happens, Uncle Walter always hears about it. He comes and tells me. I'll tell you.

HERBERT [*crossing R, below* MARGE]

No, sir! That radio stays. [*He sits on the bench.*]

JONATHAN

Disturbs Mathilda. Can't get her proper rest.

MARGE [*crossing R, to* HERBERT]

I'm sure, Mr. Rockwood, that Mr. Gage will give up his radio. Won't you, Herbert?

LOOMIS

Of course he will, under the circumstances.

JONATHAN

Then there's somethin' else.

LOOMIS
> What's that?

JONATHAN
> My privy.

HERBERT [*crossing* L, *behind* MARGE, *to* C]
> No! I draw the line there!

LOOMIS [*to* JONATHAN]
> Yes. Aren't you being unreasonable? With modern improvements in the house, there's no further use for your priv— [*He looks at* MARGE, *and corrects himself.*]—for outside plumbing.

JONATHAN
> Hold on! Who says there's no use for outside plumbin'?

LOOMIS
> Well, is there?

JONATHAN
> You better believe there is! I don't hold with inside plumbin'.

HERBERT
> But you've been using our bathroom for three months.

JONATHAN
> Yep, I have. But I ain't been happy up there.

LOOMIS
> But what do you propose to do?

JONATHAN
> Well, I propose to build the new one right where the old one was.

HERBERT

That's the front of the house now!

JONATHAN [*putting on his hat, rising*]

Mebbe I better have the doctor look at Mathilda——

HERBERT [*crossing up to the desk and sitting left of the desk*]

All right! All right!

LOOMIS

And is this the extent of your demands?

JONATHAN

I'll settle for what we said, if that's what you mean.

LOOMIS

Well, I'll get this down in writing and——

JONATHAN

Never mind 'bout that. Time enough to sign papers when you do all the things you promised.

[MATT *enters* L *and crosses to* JONATHAN.]

MATT [*to* JONATHAN]

Simpson's out front with the folding chairs.

JONATHAN [*crossing up and* R, *between the sofa and the chair*]

That so? Have him hand 'em off the wagon to you.

MATT

All right.

JONATHAN

You bring 'em in here. I'll set 'em up.

[MATT *goes out the front door.*]

HERBERT [*rising*]
Folding chairs? What are they for?

JONATHAN [*right of the desk*]
Funeral.

HERBERT
Funeral? Did somebody die?

JONATHAN
Young Charley Freeman. [*He removes his hat and places it over his heart.*] Only seventy-five.

LOOMIS [*rising*]
No. I'm sorry to hear that. Give my condolences to Charley's wife.

JONATHAN
Young Charley never married. You're thinkin' of *old* Charley. [*He crosses R, to MARGE.*] Quite a shock to old Charley—losin' his boy. [*He puts on his hat and crosses up to the front door and takes the chairs from MATT.*]

LOOMIS [*crossing up to the desk*]
Yes—well—I'm due at the office now. [*He starts to go.*]

HERBERT
Loomis! Does he have a right to hold a funeral here? In our living-room?

LOOMIS
Frankly, Mr. Gage, I don't know. I'm sure this is a case without precedent.

[LOOMIS *goes out the front door as* MATT *enters with four folding chairs, hands them to* JONATHAN, *and goes out again.*]

HERBERT

Rockwood, why are you having this funeral here?

JONATHAN

More room here. Expectin' quite a crowd.

HERBERT

Why don't you use the church?

JONATHAN

Old Charley quit the church when Reverend Smalley put electricity in. Charley says if the good Lord wanted electricity in His churches, He'd have invented it Himself. And I agree with Charley.

[MARGE *is seated on the bench.*]

HERBERT

But we have electricity *here!*

JONATHAN

This ain't a house of the Lord. Far from it!

[JONATHAN *goes out the front door for more chairs.*]

MARGE [*rising and crossing to* L C]

What can we do?

HERBERT

We can eat breakfast. I can't face a funeral on an empty stomach.

MARGE

Well, we don't have to stay here. We can go out for the day.

HERBERT

No, sir! They might decide to bury young Charley here!

[MARGE *and* HERBERT *go out* R. MATHILDA *enters* L *and sits on the sofa.* SARAH *enters at the front door with a full milk pail.*]

MATHILDA

Sarah, you ain't practiced the piano today yet.

SARAH

I'll do it, Aunt Mathilda, as soon as I've done my chores. I haven't finished Shadrach yet.

MATHILDA

Mighty nice havin' you play the piano, since I ain't up to playin' it myself any more.

SARAH

I enjoy it, Aunt Mathilda.

[SARAH *goes out* L *and closes the door.* JONATHAN *enters at the front door with more chairs.*]

JONATHAN

Feelin' some better?

MATHILDA

Some. Can't miss the services.

[UNCLE WALTER *enters at the front door.*]

UNCLE WALTER

Jon! Jon! Told everybody about the funeral and they all said they'd come.

MATHILDA

You *sure* you told everybody, Uncle Walter?

UNCLE WALTER

Yep—told everybody. [*He snaps his fingers.*] Darn it, I forgot to tell 'em who it was. [*He crosses toward the front door.*] Bet a lot of folks will be surprised.

[UNCLE WALTER *goes out the front door.*]

JONATHAN

Got good news for you, Mathilda.

MATHILDA

Seemed to me you were mighty chipper.

JONATHAN

Yep. Mr. Gage made a little deal with me.

MATHILDA

What sort of a deal?

JONATHAN

There's goin' to be some changes around here.

MATHILDA

Such as?

JONATHAN [*pointing to the radio*]

Goin' to get rid of that infernal contraption, the radio, that interferes with your rest.

MATHILDA

Don't mind it much, except maybe for the talkin' parts.

JONATHAN [*thinking*]

And that tarnation pink carpet is comin' off the steps.

MATHILDA

Kind of like that. It's nice on the feet, when I go upstairs.

JONATHAN

Won't be no need for goin' upstairs no more. ~~Now, even their lawyer sees we got the right to build a privy.~~

MATHILDA

That so?

JONATHAN

Thought you'd be pleased. [*He crosses to the sofa and glares at her.*] Suspected it all along. You *like* their indoor plumbin'.

MATHILDA

Don't feel one way or another about it.

JONATHAN [*crossing* R]

Never thought I'd live to see the day.

MATHILDA

Times change—we change with 'em. I was thinkin' awhile back, takes a funeral for you to see your old friends. I ain't seen young Charley in twenty years.

JONATHAN

Twenty-*two* years.

MATHILDA

Twenty years. Young Charley was here the day I fell down them stairs and hurt my hip. Just twenty years ago!

CURTAIN

ACT TWO

Scene Two

AT RISE OF CURTAIN: *The following January. It is late afternoon of a dark, dreary day. The converted kerosene lamp is burning on the desk.* HERBERT *is writing—trying to write.* MATT *is sitting in the most comfortable chair, right of the desk, steadfastly watching* HERBERT. HERBERT *tries to ignore* MATT'S *gaze, but he is getting more and more irritated.*]

HERBERT [*rising, carefully, slowly; this has been on his mind for a long time*]
Matt, old boy, do you mind if I ask you a question? For weeks, for months—all summer, all fall and November, December and half of January, you've been sitting in that chair—watching me. Matt, old boy, what's so fascinating about me?

MATT
Fascinating?

HERBERT
Do I remind you of somebody and you're trying to remember who? Or do you like the typewriter? Do you like to hear the click, click, click of the busy little keys?

MATT [*shaking his head*]
I don't enjoy that especially.

HERBERT
Stand up!

MATT
  What?

HERBERT
  Stand up.

  [HERBERT *crosses* R, *below* MATT. MATT *gets up, uneasily.*
  HERBERT *seizes the chair and turns it around. He gestures
  sarcastically for* MATT *to be seated.*]

HERBERT
  Set! Down! [*He crosses to the chair left of the desk.*]

MATT [*sitting, then giving the line*]
  You should've done that last summer.

  [HERBERT *goes back to the desk and sits.* MATHILDA'S *piano
  starts to pound out a loud rendition of "Brighten the Corner." * HERBERT *strides to the bedroom door and pounds on
  it. "Mrs. Rockwood, please." The piano stops. He goes back
  to the chair and sits, facing away from* MATT. MARGE *comes
  down the stairs. She is suffering from a horrible cold. She
  wears a heavy sweater over a house coat.*]

MARGE
  Darling, it's freezing in this house. [*She looks at the therm-
  ostat on the back wall.*] It's dropped ten degrees since lunch.
  [*She crosses* R, *to the radiator, under the window* U C.]

HERBERT
  There's nothing I can do about it.

MARGE
  Can't we have a little more heat? [*She feels the radiator.*]

HERBERT

Marge, will you please stop going around feeling radiators!

MARGE

That's what keeps them as warm as they are. [*She sees* MATT *sitting in the misplaced chair.*] Oh, Matt!

MATT [*rising, questioningly*]

Yes, Mrs. Gage?

[MARGE *takes the chair and swings it back to its former position. She pats it invitingly.* MATT *sits down.*]

MARGE

Herbert.

[HERBERT *turns to the desk, sees* MATT *in his old position, glares, exhales, and throws his paper away.*]

MARGE

We've simply got to have more heat. Darling, we're not living in an apartment in New York now. You can't just pound on the radiator and—presto! The superintendent turns on the heat. Herbert, *you're* our *super!*

HERBERT

Kindly do not refer to me as our super. [*He resumes his typing.*]

MARGE

Well, you are! It's up to you to keep us from freezing to death. Heavens! [*She crosses* D L, *to above the sofa.*] The way you used to swear at the super on Sixty-fifth Street.

HERBERT

I never swore at him.

MARGE [standing above the sofa]

Oh, you used to curse him to China and back!

HERBERT [rising]

I didn't. He had a very difficult job and I sympathized with him. He was right about a lot of things—too much heat *is* unhealthy. Sixty—[He sneaks a look at the thermostat.]— Sixty-one is a sensible temperature. [He sits in the chair left of the desk.]

[MATT sees the Gorley boy pass the window. He starts for the front door. There is a knock.]

MARGE

Who is it, Matt?

MATT

Somebody for me, Mrs. Gage.

MARGE [calling after him]

Matt, put on a coat—or you'll catch cold, too.

MATT

It ain't so bad out.

[MATT goes out the front door.]

MARGE [to HERBERT]

Darling, I'm going to fix dinner for all of you, then go back to bed. Are the groceries in the kitchen or did you leave them in the car?

HERBERT

What groceries?

MARGE

Herbert! I gave you the list and you put it in your pocket!

HERBERT

I didn't put anything in my pocket.

MARGE [*taking the list out of his pocket, handing it to him*]
What's that?

HERBERT

I've been framed.

MARGE

I don't want any dinner, so why don't you take the children
in to the restaurant to eat?

HERBERT

If you don't mind being left alone.

MARGE

Not at all. If you'll build a fire in the fireplace before you go.

HERBERT

I'll do it right away.

MARGE [*starting for the stairs*]
I'm going back to bed.

HERBERT [*on his way to the kitchen*]
I'll get Paula to help me get some wood.

MARGE [*at the foot of the stairs*]
Bundle up!

[MARGE *goes up the stairs.* HERBERT *starts to go out* R. MA-
THILDA *enters* L, *crosses to the pegs, and puts on an over-
coat.*]

MATHILDA

Good evenin', Mr. Gage.

HERBERT

Good evening. It's getting pretty nasty out, Mrs. Rockwood.
I wouldn't go out if I were you.

MATHILDA

Oh, I'm not goin' out!

[MATHILDA *goes up the stairs.* HERBERT *goes out* R. *After a
moment's pause,* MATT *comes back in the front door. He is
perturbed. After hesitating a second, he looks through the
kitchen door. Then he goes to the stairs and calls softly.*]

MATT

Mrs. Gage—Mrs. Gage . . .

[BARBARA *comes down the stairs.*]

BARBARA

Mother's taking some aspirin and going to bed, Matt.

MATT

Oh, she is. [*This makes him more worried.*]

BARBARA

Maybe it's something I can do.

MATT [*shaking his head*]

I don't think so.

BARBARA

Well, what is it?

MATT

Your mother's sick, huh?

BARBARA

She feels dreadful. Can't you tell me, Matt?

MATT

It's Mrs. Gorley. Her time's come sooner than she expected.

BARBARA

You mean she's having her baby?

MATT [*nodding*]

And she's all alone—except for her five little ones. The biggest was just here. He was crying. He's only eight.

BARBARA

Where's her husband?

MATT

He's in town. He ain't back yet.

BARBARA [*crossing to the desk*]

Matt, we've got to get a doctor.

MATT [*crossing up to* BARBARA]

Can't. Little Melvin Gorley took a note from his ma to Mrs. Tuttle, but the Tuttles weren't home. He got in, though, and used their phone. Old Doc Lippert's on a case, and he's the only doctor this side of Danbury.

BARBARA

We've got to do something. . . .

MATT [*crossing* R]

My ma ain't spry enough any more to get back through them woods to the Gorleys'. I thought maybe *your* mother—but you say she's sick.

BARBARA

We mustn't tell Mother! She'd do it, and with her cold it'd

mean pneumonia for her. If only Mrs. Tuttle were home . . . [*She pauses, thinking, then:*] Matt!

MATT

Huh?

BARBARA

I've thought of somebody!

MATT

Who?

BARBARA

Me! Me!

MATT

You ever done it?

BARBARA

No. But I took a Red Cross course, and maybe Mrs. Gorley might be able to help a little.

[MATT *looks at her quizzically.*]

BARBARA

Well, I know *something!* I've been reading Life Magazine since I was ten years old.

MATT

I think maybe you better see if your mother will let you.

BARBARA

She wouldn't! So we mustn't ask her. [*She turns, looks out the window* U C, *and then crosses up to the window.*] Matt, isn't there a quicker way than back through the woods?

MATT

Not walking. Of course, if we had a car.

BARBARA [*grabbing* MATT'S *arm and pushing him toward the front door*]

We do! Matt, you back it out of the garage and wait for me in it. Oh, golly!

MATT

If you're afraid . . .

BARBARA

I'm not afraid! I hope it's a boy! [*She runs upstairs.*] I'll pack a bag—my first-aid kit, some towels, hot water, some sheets——

MATT [*crossing to the stairs*]

Maybe we better leave a note.

[BARBARA *disappears at the head of the stairs.* MATT *gets his hat and coat and goes out the front door quickly. After a moment,* MATHILDA *comes down the stairs.*]

MATHILDA [*calling*]

Jonathan! Jonathan!

JONATHAN [*offstage*]

Yeah, I'm comin'.

[JONATHAN *enters* R.]

MATHILDA

Jonathan, when you get a minute, will you take them empty jars down to the cellar for me?

JONATHAN

Yeh.

MATHILDA [*above the sofa*]

Gettin' too hot in our room. Thought I'd leave the door open for a second.

JONATHAN [*crossing L*]

Ain't too hot out here. It's cold. Mighty cold.

MATHILDA

It is, ain't it? [*She folds her arms.*] Measured their oil this mornin'. Nearly gone. Uncle Walter was tellin' me there's been a fuel oil famine around here every winter for the past four or five years.

JONATHAN

That ain't it! Plenty oil. Democrats down in Washington! [*He pauses.*] Goin' to punish New England for votin' Republican!

MATHILDA [*mildly*]

Don't look very Christian to me. Jonathan, it seems to me you might offer to help Gage a little.

JONATHAN

If Gage weren't so stubborn, weren't so durn bull-headed to ask my advice, I could save 'em a lot of trouble. A lot.

MATHILDA

I guess you could.

JONATHAN

Know I could.

MATHILDA

Where's Matt? [*She crosses up, and looks upstairs.*]

JONATHAN

Saw him around an hour or so ago. He's around someplace.

MATHILDA

How's the weather?

JONATHAN

Peculiar. Somethin's comin'. Don't know what, but somethin'. Never seen a more ornery lookin' sky. And it's mighty
cold out.

[MATHILDA *goes out* L *and closes the door.* JONATHAN *but-
tons up his jacket and starts to cross* R, *putting on his mit-
tens. He thinks of how cold it is outside, turns back, looks at
the bedroom door, and then sneaks upstairs. Immediately,*
BARBARA *hurries down the stairs, carrying a suitcase, and
goes out the front door. She is hardly through the door when*
SARAH *comes stealthily down the stairs and watches her
through the stair window.* HERBERT *and* PAULA *enter* R. *They
are carrying firewood, which is very crumbly, very scrawny.
They dump it on the hearth.*]

HERBERT

Now, Paula, I want you to help me get some paper and some
matches.

PAULA

All right.

[PAULA *comes to the desk and sees* SARAH. *On* SARAH'S *face
is a beatific, ecstatic smile.*]

PAULA

What's eating you, Sarah?

SARAH

Nothing. Nothing, whatsoever. [*She sits smugly in the chair left of the desk.*]

[JONATHAN *starts down the stairs.*]

HERBERT

Hurry up, Paula.

PAULA

Yes, sir.

[HERBERT *busies himself with the fire.* PAULA *crosses with paper and matches from the desk.*]

PAULA

Let me do it, Pop. Please, huh?

HERBERT

You watch. In case you ever have to do it when I'm not around.

[JONATHAN *crosses to the door* L *and slams it, walking non-chalantly* R.]

JONATHAN

Buildin' a fire?

HERBERT [*carefully*]

Yes, I'm building a fire.

JONATHAN [*after a pause*]

Ever build a fire before?

HERBERT

Lots of times.

JONATHAN [*another pause*]
Any fire you ever build ever burn?

HERBERT [*grimly*]
This one will.

JONATHAN
With that wood you got there? [*He shakes his head.*]

HERBERT
And this is the kind of wood you should use.

JONATHAN
Won't burn.

HERBERT
It'll burn if you know how to use it.

JONATHAN
Got to cut your wood in the summer, so it'll dry out. Green wood won't burn. Next spring I'll——

HERBERT
I wouldn't make any plans about next spring if I were you. Chances are you won't be here next spring.

JONATHAN
That so? [*He sits on the bench.*] Ain't seen your lawyer around lately. He get himself arrested and put in jail?

HERBERT [*wearily, sitting on the bench*]
Rockwood, I don't know why you are so stubborn about this. I should think you and your wife would be much more comfortable in a little place of your own. Where you wouldn't be bothered by us.

[JONATHAN *chuckles.*]

HERBERT

What's funny?

JONATHAN

Didn't think you could figure out any more new arguments. Thought you'd used 'em all up.

HERBERT

Well, it's true! It must be terrible for you to have a couple of noisy kids tearing around the house all the time.

JONATHAN

Me and Mathilda like young folks.

HERBERT

All right, but you don't like *me!* Think how wonderful it'd be not to have to see me every day.

JONATHAN

Tell you the truth, Gage, I ain't especially fond of you. You got some mighty queer and aggravatin' traits. But I figure you're young yet. You might be a pretty pleasant human bein' ten, fifteen years from now. Yep, and Mathilda and me will be glad to have you around the place.

HERBERT [*exasperated, rising and shouting*]

Rockwood, can't you get it through that head of yours that——

JONATHAN [*rising and crossing* U R]

Hmm. On second thought—make it twenty, twenty-five years.

[JONATHAN *goes out* R, *chuckling. The front door bursts open.* GEORGE *enters. He has a gaudy florist box and a suitcase and is in great high spirits.*]

GEORGE

Hey, I'm here! Lo, the bridegroom cometh!

[PAULA *and* HERBERT *rush to greet him.*]

HERBERT

This is wonderful, George, wonderful!

PAULA

Gee! It's George!

GEORGE

Say, you seem surprised to see me.

HERBERT

We are!

GEORGE

I sent Barbara a telegram. I'm out! Took my finals when this quarter ended. I passed. Got my degree. Where's Barbara? [*He lays the florist box and his hat on the table* R.]

HERBERT

Around someplace. Paula——

PAULA

I'll find her.

[PAULA *dashes up the stairs.*]

GEORGE

You didn't get my wire, huh? [*He crosses* L *and throws his coat on the newel post.*] You farmers! I thought I'd find the joint jumping—orange blossoms, bridesmaids! [*He is still at the foot of the stairs.*] Hey, Barbara! [*He crosses R, back to* HERBERT.] Look, it's still all right, isn't it? I got a job! In Philadelphia! Is it all right if I take your daughter to Philadelphia? We *can* get married right away, can't we? You know you promised, Barbara promised. Even *I* promised!

HERBERT [*laughing*]
There's going to be a wedding.

GEORGE [*shaking hands with* HERBERT]
There's going to be a wedding! I'm going to get married!

[MARGE, *bundled up, hurries down the stairs.* PAULA *is behind her.*]

MARGE
George! It's you!

[GEORGE *crosses L, to kiss her.*]

MARGE
No, don't kiss me! I've got a cold and I don't want Barbara to catch it!

GEORGE
I wired but you didn't get it! I rented a car. It's outside. I got a room at the New Yorker for Barbara and me tonight. I got money saved and a job in Philadelphia! I got everything! Where is Barbara?

PAULA [*on the stairs*]
She isn't up here, George.

HERBERT

Well, she isn't down here.

MARGE

If she were in the house, she would have heard you, you maniac!

GEORGE

I'm a lonely man. I want to see the bride.

[MARGE *turns to* SARAH, *who has adopted a policy of watchful waiting.*]

MARGE

Sarah, do you know where Barbara is?

SARAH [*rising from the desk and crossing* D L, *to below the sofa, too elaborately casual*]

No—no, I have no idea whatsoever where she is. [*She turns and finds them all looking at her.*] What are you all looking at me for? I *don't* know!

GEORGE [*to* HERBERT]

She knows something!

HERBERT

Yep.

[GEORGE *crosses to* SARAH.]

GEORGE

Look, Sarah, Barbara *did* get my wire, huh? And she's pulling some kind of a joke—she's going to surprise me somehow. C'mon, tell me.

[SARAH *shakes her head and sits on the sofa.*]

HERBERT
Sarah!

MARGE
Darling, tell George! Can't you see he's worried?

GEORGE [*kneeling beside her*]
I won't spoil it. I promise to be surprised. I'll be astounded!

SARAH
You'd be astounded all right! [*She grits her teeth.*] But I won't tell you.

PAULA [*coming to* L C]
Hey! Want me to twist her wrist?

[GEORGE *rises and crosses* L, *to behind the sofa.*]

HERBERT [*crossing* L, *below* MARGE]
In one second, I'll do worse than that if she doesn't——

SARAH [*facing front*]
You can beat me to within an inch of my life and my lips will remain sealed! Forever!

HERBERT
Sarah, I'm warning you for the last time——

SARAH
You can torture me! Put me on the rack! Stake me to an ant-hill! But I shall never tell you.

HERBERT
Dammit, Sarah——

MARGE [*crossing* L, *below* HERBERT, *to the sofa, and sitting*]
Herbert, let me handle this. You'll only make her more stubborn.

[HERBERT *eases* R. PAULA *eases up to the window* U C.
MARGE *sits beside* SARAH, *quietly.*]

MARGE
Sarah, you've never told me a lie, have you?

SARAH
No.

MARGE
And you're never going to tell me a lie, are you?

[HERBERT *crosses up to the right of the desk.*]

SARAH
As long as you remain honest with me, Mother, I shall remain honest with you.

PAULA
Hey! Our car's gone!

HERBERT
It is? Sarah, enough of this nonsense!

MARGE
Did Barbara go someplace in the car?

SARAH
Yes. [*She catches herself.*]

GEORGE
Did she know I was coming? Did she go to meet me? [*He speaks violently.*] Answer me! Did Barbara——

SARAH [*suddenly frightened*]
No! [*She rises, and crosses up back of the chair right of the sofa. She faces upstage.*] I don't care, now! It's too late and you can't stop them! [*She turns downstage.*] By now it's all over—and *I know* they'll be very, very happy together!

[*They are all stricken silent with amazement.*]

HERBERT [*finally*]
Sarah, who—who——

[JONATHAN *enters* R.]

JONATHAN
Any you folks seen Matt? Suppertime, and——

HERBERT [*in agony*]
Matt!

JONATHAN
—he ain't never been late to supper. [*He remains standing by the door* L.]

HERBERT [*groaning*]
Not Matt—no, not Matt . . .

[MARGE *rises and crosses* R, *to* HERBERT.]

GEORGE [*crossing* R, *to* SARAH]
Did Barbara run away with Matt?

SARAH
Yes!

JONATHAN
What's that?

GEORGE

Did Barbara tell you she was going to marry Matt? How do you *know* about it?

SARAH

I saw her sneak out with her suitcase. I saw them get in the car together—and go away.

MARGE [*hopefully*]

Aren't we jumping to conclusions, maybe?

HERBERT [*roaring*]

What else could it be?

[MATHILDA *enters* L *and stands on the step.*]

MARGE

Oh, Herbert! [*She crosses up and begins to cry.*]

GEORGE [*crossing* R, *hotly, to* HERBERT]

I warned you about that guy—I warned you!

HERBERT

I tried to keep them apart. I didn't let Barbara even talk to him.

GEORGE

Yeah! And you see what you did? It made him attractive as the devil to her.

SARAH

Of course—forbidden fruit. [*She crosses her arms.*]

GEORGE [*to* SARAH, *crossing* L]

You could've stopped them, Sarah.

[MARGE *crosses down.*]

SARAH

I didn't want to stop them. [*She crosses* R, *to* MARGE.] I thought if they got married it would solve everything around here. Matt would be Daddy's son-in-law. [*She crosses up to right of the desk.*]

HERBERT [*crossing* D R, *to the rocker, and sitting*]

Oh, no!

MATHILDA

Jonathan! Is it what I think it is? Barbara and our Mattie-boy gettin' married?

JONATHAN

Seems so.

MATHILDA [*beaming*]

Well! Isn't that fine!

MARGE [*crossing* L, *to* MATHILDA]

What—what did you say, Mrs. Rockwood?

MATHILDA

Always knew that some day Matt would find himself a nice girl.

JONATHAN

Don't know 'bout that.

MARGE [*indignantly, crossing* L, *to* JONATHAN]

You don't know if Barbara is a nice girl?

JONATHAN

Looks to me like Matt was lured into it.

MARGE

Really, Mr.——

HERBERT [crossing L]
What are you——

MATHILDA [crossing R, to HERBERT]
Now, now. Ain't nothin' like settlin' down with a good man to take the wildness out of a girl. [She crosses L, to between JONATHAN and MARGE.] Jonathan! Wonder if I could find them baby pictures of Mattie. [She starts toward her room.] I'm sure Mr. and Mrs. Gage would enjoy seeing them.

HERBERT
Mrs. Rockwood, don't go to a lot of trouble on our account. Please!

SARAH
Can I help you, Aunt Mathilda?

MATHILDA
Come along.

[The lights go out just as SARAH and MATHILDA go out L.]

PAULA
Hey, the lights!

[PAULA crosses up and pulls the plug on the desk lamp.]

HERBERT
Damn!

JONATHAN [crossing up]
Storm probably tore down the wires.

MARGE
Herbert, what will we do?

HERBERT

They'll come back on in a minute.

JONATHAN

Never did hold with electricity. Fails you.

PAULA

Look, there's a light in the Rockwoods' room!

JONATHAN

Yep. We don't use no modern improvements.

[MATHILDA *and* SARAH *enter* L, *each with an oil lamp.* MA-
THILDA *places hers on the table* D L. SARAH *places hers on
the desk, and crosses up and sits on the window seat left of
the desk.* PAULA *sits in the chair right of the desk.*]

MATHILDA [*as she enters*]

Jonathan, we can get along with just one of our lamps.

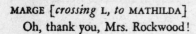

MARGE [*crossing* L, *to* MATHILDA]

Oh, thank you, Mrs. Rockwood!

JONATHAN [*to* HERBERT]

Too bad, Gage. Your electric oil furnace won't work without
electricity. [*He turns to* MARGE.] And you'll have to get
along without your kitchen stove, too. And your electric ice-
box and your electric sweeper, and——[*He looks closely at*
HERBERT.] Too bad you didn't shave 'fore the storm hit us.
Can't now.

[HERBERT *rubs his chin.*]

JONATHAN

'Course one good thing. Your plumbin' won't freeze.

MARGE

Oh, it won't! Well, that's something.

JONATHAN [*starting to cross* R]

No power for your pump. Won't be any water any place in the plumbin' to freeze.

MARGE

No water!

MATHILDA

Jonathan, can you help me get into the big box for them pictures of Mattie?

JONATHAN

Nope, the storm's about to hit us. I'm goin' out to the barn and take a look at my stock. [*He crosses* R.]

MATHILDA

Make sure they're plenty warm. It's goin' to freeze.

[MATHILDA *goes out* L.]

JONATHAN

Know it is. [*He stops at the door* R, *crosses down by the fireplace, and turns to* HERBERT.] Gage, about Matt and Barbara. What's got to be has got to be. But there's one thing I want understood right now. Don't want no grandchildren runnin' around here by the name of *Herbert.*

[JONATHAN *goes out* R.]

HERBERT

Marge, shall I go down to the Simpsons' and phone the police? Maybe they could locate Barbara before it's too late.

GEORGE [*who is sitting in the chair left of the desk*]

Don't do it for me. If she wants to marry that guy, well—
she wants to marry that guy.

[HERBERT *sits on the sofa.*]

MARGE [*crossing* L]

George, don't . . .

GEORGE

I'm going back to New York. [*He rises.*]

MARGE

No, George, please . . .

GEORGE

Yeah, I better get started. It's storming out.

MARGE

But if we want to get in touch with you, if anything——

GEORGE [*getting his coat and bag*]

I don't know where I'll be. Honest, I don't, Mrs. Gage.
That thing in Philadelphia would be a lousy job without
Barbara around. Maybe I'll go back to California. I've got
friends out there. [*He starts putting on his coat.*] Look,
maybe I don't want you to get in touch with me for a while.
[*He crosses* R, *below* MARGE.] You understand, don't you,
Mrs. Gage?

MARGE

George, you can't leave now. It's turned into a blizzard. Stay
overnight, anyway.

GEORGE

Well—all right.

[MATHILDA *enters* L *with a thick, old-fashioned plush-covered album. She crosses to the sofa and sits beside* HERBERT.]

MATHILDA

Here it is! I found it! Here's Mattie when he was three months old. Just look at him laugh! What are you laughing at, Mattie-boy?

[HERBERT *cringes.* MATHILDA *turns the page.*]

MATHILDA

And here's his first tooth! [*She holds up a tooth on a red ribbon.*]

[HERBERT *turns his back on her.* JONATHAN *enters* R, *carrying two little pigs. If real pigs are not available, he can pretend to carry them in a basket.*]

JONATHAN

Too cold in the barn for these little pigs. They'll have to stay in here. [*He puts the pigs on the floor at* C.]

HERBERT [*climbing up on the sofa*]

Pigs, too!

CURTAIN

ACT THREE

AT RISE OF CURTAIN: *It is early the next morning. The table* R *has been turned to run up- and downstage. It is partially set for breakfast. The bench is right of the table, and there is a chair left of it. The small stool is downstage of the table.* PAULA *and* SARAH, *bundled up against the elements of the living-room, are at the fireplace.* PAULA *is using* MARGE'S *antique bellows on the smoldering fire, without success.* SARAH *is waiting her turn.*]

SARAH
It's my turn now.

PAULA
Wait a minute!

SARAH
You act as if those were your bellows! Honestly, Paula!

PAULA [*disgustedly*]
Here, take them. [*She crosses to the stool and sits.*]

[MARGE *enters from the kitchen,* R. *She has on a heavy coat, and a scarf over her head. She takes dishes to the table, and starts setting it.*]

MARGE
Will we be able to make coffee on that fire?

PAULA [*bitterly*]
Ice coffee, maybe.

135

MARGE

If only your father weren't so——I bet Mr. Rockwood would give us some of his nice logs if he would only ask for them. [*She shakes her head in despair.*] Where *is* your father?

SARAH

Helping George dig out his car.

MARGE

Well, breakfast will soon be ready—such as it is.

SARAH

Isn't there anyplace we could buy something?

MARGE

You know everything is closed around here on Sunday. [*She brightens.*] Well! Have you two washed your hands?

PAULA

It's too cold to take our gloves off.

SARAH

And there isn't any water.

MARGE

There isn't anything—anything at all.

[MARGE *goes out* R.]

SARAH [*looking after her*]
Poor woman.

PAULA

Huh?

SARAH

She cried almost all last night. Couldn't you hear her?

PAULA
  No. Father kept me awake.

SARAH [*surprised*]
  Crying?

PAULA [*facing front, shaking her head*]
  No, swearing.

  [MARGE *enters* R *with a chair, which she places at the head of the table.*]

MARGE
  Paula, rap on the window for your father and George.

  [PAULA *crosses to the window* U C *and raps, motioning to the men outside.*]

MARGE
  Don't bother with those bellows any more, Sarah. It isn't doing any good.

  [SARAH *deserts the bellows.*]

SARAH [*crossing to between the table and the bench*]
  I'm starving!

MARGE
  We all are, dear.

SARAH
  Mother?

MARGE
  Yes?

SARAH
  Can't Barbara's marriage be annulled?

MARGE

No, Sarah. I don't think so. Darling, let's not talk about it just now, shall we?

[HERBERT *enters at the front door.*]

MARGE

Where's George, dear?

HERBERT

He doesn't want any breakfast. He wants to get going. [*He crosses* L, *with bluff heartiness.*] Well, there's nothing like shovelling snow before breakfast to make a man——Say, I smell coffee! [*He takes a deep, appreciative breath.*] Most wonderful smell in the world. [*He crosses* R, *to left of the desk, to* MARGE.] How could you make coffee? [*He realizes she couldn't. Slowly, he turns and looks daggers at the Rockwoods' room.*] No wonder he's so bilious. Drinks coffee all the time.

MARGE [*inhaling wistfully*]

It does smell good, doesn't it?

HERBERT [*sternly*]

Marge!

MARGE

Yes, Herbert——come, children.

[*They all sit down at the table.* SARAH *and* PAULA *sit on the bench,* SARAH *upstage, while* HERBERT *sits above and* MARGE *sits left of the table.*]

SARAH [*to* HERBERT]

Shall I say grace?

HERBERT [*looking over the table*]
  For corn flakes—and stuffed olives?

MARGE
  They aren't stuffed.

HERBERT
  Isn't there anything else?

MARGE
  I'm sorry, Herbert.

HERBERT [*brightly*]
  Well, I'll have some corn flakes. Somebody pass the milk.

MARGE
  This isn't milk. It's molasses. I thought maybe on the corn
  flakes it might——

HERBERT
  Marge—please!

MARGE [*helplessly*]
  Well . . .

  [*There is a despondent pause. Then* MARGE *straightens,
  brightens, and smiles.*]

MARGE
  Well!

  [MARGE *shakes out her napkin, busily spreads it on her lap,
  straightens her silverware, and picks up the olive dish. With
  a charming smile she hands it to* PAULA, *who quickly passes
  it on to* SARAH *without even looking at the damn things.*
  SARAH *just as quickly passes it on to* HERBERT, *who passes it*

back to MARGE, *who is surprised to get it back so quickly. She places the dish before her. Everybody is watching her. She smiles at them, decorously picks up an olive, takes a bite out of it, and thoroughly enjoys it.*]

HERBERT [*his voice horrible with menace*]
I'm warning you, Marge, if you say it's delicious, I'll strangle you.

[*There is a pause.*]

PAULA [*to* SARAH]
I read a story once. Some miners were trapped in a mine for seventy-two days. They ate coal.

MARGE [*getting even with* HERBERT]
We don't have any coal.

SARAH
Which is quicker—I mean, which will happen first? [*She faces front.*] Will I freeze to death or starve to death?

MARGE
Now, darling.

[JONATHAN *stamps in from* R *and crosses* L, *swinging an empty bucket.* SARAH *rises and crosses toward him.*]

SARAH
Good morning, Uncle Jonathan!

JONATHAN
Mornin', Sarah.

SARAH [*crossing* L, *to right of the desk*]
What have you been doing?

JONATHAN

Feedin' the pigs. Should've seen them little rascals eat!

[JONATHAN *goes out* L.]

SARAH [*facing front*]

I wish I *was* a pig!

HERBERT

I wish I *were* a pig. Sit down.

[SARAH *crosses to the table and sits.*]

HERBERT [*sternly*]

Eat your olives!

SARAH

I don't like olives!

HERBERT

If you don't eat your olives, you can't have any molasses!

SARAH [*to* HERBERT]

I detest molasses!

PAULA

Sarah!

SARAH [*to* PAULA]

I don't care. I think he's cruel! Letting his wife and children die of starvation and exposure when there's food and plenty right in there! [*She points to the Rockwoods' room.*]

HERBERT

Be quiet! [*He rises.*] If ever we accept anything from them, if we ever become obligated to them——No, no, by Heaven!

[JONATHAN *enters* L, *closes the door, crosses* R, *and goes out* R.]

HERBERT [*as* JONATHAN *comes in*]
Rockwood, do you have to keep barging in and out? Can't a man even enjoy his breakfast in peace?

[JONATHAN *is gone.*]

HERBERT [*directly to* MARGE]
I'm going to fire that lawyer of yours! What's he doing? Nothing! I'm going to hire a *crooked* lawyer!

[PAULA *and* SARAH *start forward.* HERBERT *sits.*]

MARGE
Herbert, the children . ▪ ▪

HERBERT
Damn!

MARGE [*helplessly*]
It's all my fault. I thought the Rockwoods were dead.

HERBERT
They'll outlive us!

PAULA [*gloomily*]
I'm not sure—but I think I'm beginning to get weaker already. [*She brightens.*] I'm going to start keeping a diary!

MARGE [*tearfully*]
And now Barbara!

HERBERT
Now, Marge, don't——

SARAH

Mother, you and Father decided not to discuss Barbara in front of the children.

[JONATHAN *enters* R *and crosses* L *with two hams and a fine slab of bacon. The Gage family silently watch him walk through the living-room. He goes out* L.]

HERBERT [*after the door has closed*]

Hoarder! Republican hoarder!

MARGE

Just because *he* was foresighted enough to——

HERBERT

Are you insinuating that I——Who begged you to shop ahead? Who begged you to buy by the case?

MARGE [*rising*]

I did! I did buy a case.

HERBERT

A case of what?

MARGE

Olives.

[GEORGE *enters at the front door.*]

GEORGE [*crossing* D C]

I've got it dug out enough, I think. [*He shivers.*] Gee, it's cold in here! The snow plows are working their way up the hill. So I ought to be able to get out of here any minute now.

MARGE [*crossing toward him*]

George, I do wish you'd tell us where you'll be.

GEORGE

I don't know. Really, I don't, Mrs. Gage.

[SARAH *rises and crosses* L, *to* GEORGE, *between* MARGE *and* GEORGE. MARGE *eases* R.]

SARAH

George! I'm sorry, George. I didn't think. I could kill my-self with pleasure.

PAULA [*going to the stool from the bench, and sitting*]
Want a loan of my Girl Scout knife?

GEORGE [*grinning at* SARAH]
Listen—Sarah.

SARAH

I'm listening.

GEORGE

If you had stopped them by yelling, you wouldn't have stopped Barbara from *wanting* to marry him. Would you?

SARAH

No.

GEORGE

No. See what I mean?

SARAH [*nodding*]
Her heart belongs to another.

GEORGE

Correct. And it could never belong to me.

[GEORGE *goes up the stairs, and looks out the stair window as there is a knock on the front door.*]

PAULA

  I'll get it.

SARAH

  No, let me.

  [SARAH *and* PAULA *race for it.* SARAH *wins, and opens the door for* CARSON. SARAH *pushes* PAULA, *who falls into* HER-BERT.]

CARSON

  Good morning. Your folks home? [*He crosses down to the chair right of the desk.*] My name's Carson, Mr. Gage. I'm the man who talked to you on the phone last night, about your daughter.

HERBERT [*rising*]

  Oh, yes, Mr. Carson.

CARSON [*noticing their overcoats*]

  About to go out some place?

HERBERT

  No, no. Any news of Barbara?

CARSON

  Barbara. That's your daughter.

HERBERT

  Of course!

CARSON

  I couldn't hear you very well on the phone. You know Saturday night around a jail. Pretty noisy.

MARGE [*crossing* R]

  You haven't found Barbara, have you?

CARSON

Well, not yet.

HERBERT

Not yet! Heaven knows where she is by now.

MARGE

Or what's happened to her! Surely, Mr. Carson, you can understand how anxious we are.

CARSON [*crossing* L, *below* MARGE, *to left of the desk*]

Mrs. Gage, if I may take the liberty. You know, I seen a lot of elopements in my time, and seventy, seventy-five percent of them turned out for the best. Now, in this case, I happen to know Matt Rockwood, and, fundamentally, Matt's a nice person. No doubt about it he'll make a good husband, and getting married might just keep him out of trouble.

HERBERT

Carson! Listen!

CARSON [*crossing* R, *to* HERBERT, *quickly*]

I know how you feel. It's natural. But you've got to look at it this way. [*He turns to* MARGE.] You won't be losing a daughter. [*He turns to* HERBERT.] You'll be gaining a son.

HERBERT

We already had Matt! [*He sits in the chair above the table, sneezes, and puts on his cap.*]

CARSON [*to* HERBERT]

Mr. Gage, marriage is a serious business, and I'd hate to see you and the missus make a mistake.

HERBERT

Carson, never mind! We'll go to the State Police. They'll find her for me.

CARSON [*hastily*]

Oh, no, I couldn't let you do that! If you really want your daughter back, I'm your man. [*He crosses* D R, *to the mantel.*] This is a photo of Barbara?

MARGE

Yes.

CARSON [*taking down the photo*]

Mind if I borrow it? Might come in handy.

MARGE

Not at all.

CARSON

Nice-looking girl.

MARGE

Oh, thank you.

CARSON [*crossing up, to above the table, looking at the picture again*]

You know—they'd make a real cute couple.

HERBERT

Carson, will you please——

CARSON

All right, all right. I don't want to keep you from your - [*He looks down at the table, questioningly.*]—breakfast.

HERBERT [*savagely*]

Yes!

CARSON [*crossing up and opening the front door*]
No wonder she eloped!

[CARSON *goes out the front door.*]

MARGE
He didn't seem very efficient, did he, Herbert?

HERBERT
You can't tell. Sometimes small-town police surprise you.

[*There is a knock off* R.]

SARAH
Somebody's knocking at the kitchen door!

[SARAH *and* PAULA *race into the kitchen,* R.]

MARGE
Herbert! The door's locked! Maybe it's Barbara!

HERBERT
Now, don't be silly. What would Barbara be doing at the
back door?

[HERBERT *and* MARGE *look into the kitchen.* GEORGE *is coming down the stairs. He carries his suitcase.*]

MARGE [*looking off, disappointed*]
It's the little Trimble boy.

[SARAH *and* PAULA *rush back on from* R.]

SARAH [*waving a telegram*]
A telegram! A telegram!

PAULA
From Barbara, I bet! I bet anything!

MARGE

Oh, thank Heavens!

HERBERT

Give it to me.

[MARGE *opens the wire and hands it to* HERBERT, *who hands it to* GEORGE.]

MARGE

Oh, dear! . . .

GEORGE

What's it say? [*He takes the telegram and reads aloud.*] "Arriving today. Start ringing the wedding bells. George." [*There is a pause. He crosses* L, *picks up his suitcase, and starts* R.] Well, good-bye, everybody.

HERBERT

George, I don't know what to say.

[PAULA *sits on the bench.*]

GEORGE

It's all right. It's going to be all right. Let's not——Well, so long. So long, everybody!

[SARAH *crosses to* GEORGE.]

SARAH [*like in the movies*]

Good-bye, George—don't do anything desperate!

HERBERT

Oh, for Heaven's sake!

GEORGE

So long!

[GEORGE *goes out the front door.*]

MARGE

I had my heart set on Barbara and that boy. He came here to get married and he didn't even get a cup of coffee.

HERBERT

Will you stop talking about coffee.

PAULA [*now sitting on the bench, writing in a notebook*]
Dad! How much do you weigh right now?

HERBERT

What? Huh?

PAULA

I want to make a record of all our weights at the beginning and at the end.

HERBERT

Stop it, now, stop it!

SARAH [*suddenly excited, crossing between the bench and the fireplace, to the cupboard*]
Say! I know something—I know where there's something to eat!

MARGE

Where? What are you talking about?

SARAH

You'll see! Barbara had this all ready to send to George! Daddy was supposed to mail it the next time he went to town! [*She takes a box from the cupboard above the fireplace.*]

HERBERT [*crossing* R, *to the table*]
Give it to me, give it to me!

[HERBERT *takes it from her, puts it on the table, and wrenches off the string. Everybody gathers around and watches, their tongues hanging out.* SARAH *shoots her hand into the box.*]

HERBERT
Keep your hands out! [*He slaps her hand.*] You'll get your share!

[PAULA *is kneeling on the bench.* SARAH *is standing downstage of* PAULA. HERBERT *is sitting on the stool below the table.* HERBERT *pulls out a record album, and hands it to* PAULA.]

HERBERT
Records! [*He fumbles excitedly in the box.*] Here's something! Here's something!

PAULA
Quick, Daddy, quick!

[HERBERT *unwraps the package. He is holding a large jar of olives. He hands it disgustedly to* MARGE. MARGE *crosses up above the table, puts the olives on the table, and crosses down by the fireplace and shuts the cupboard door.* UNCLE WALTER *stamps in at the front door without knocking and crosses to the door* L *without looking at the Gages. He raps on the Rockwoods' door.*]

JONATHAN [*offstage*]
Yeh?

UNCLE WALTER

Just goin' by, Jon.

[JONATHAN *opens the door* L.]

UNCLE WALTER

I thought I'd stop in to say good mornin'.

JONATHAN

Mornin', Uncle Walter.

UNCLE WALTER

Mornin'. Well, guess I better be gettin' home. [*He turns abruptly and starts to cross* R.]

[MATHILDA *hurries in* L.]

MATHILDA

Uncle Walter, won't you have a bit of breakfast with us?

UNCLE WALTER

Nope. Thanks.

MATHILDA

There's bacon—or mebbe you'd like fried ham better. And fried potatoes. Coffee—good, hot coffee. And then I made a big batch of biscuits.

JONATHAN

You know Mathilda's biscuits.

UNCLE WALTER

Best I ever tasted.

JONATHAN

Melt in your mouth. Fresh-made butter and honey.

MATHILDA

Or mebbe you like preserves on 'em.

[PAULA *is slowly rising, a table knife above her head.*]

MARGE

Paula! Give me that knife! [*She takes it from her.*]

JONATHAN

Course you'll stay, Uncle Walter.

UNCLE WALTER [*shaking his head*]
Had my breakfast.

MATHILDA

What did you have?

UNCLE WALTER

Sausages, fried eggs, maple syrup, coffee.

MATHILDA

Now, Uncle Walter, you don't call that a breakfast for a
man!

UNCLE WALTER

Nope. Wasn't hungry! [*He starts* R *again, and pauses at* C.]
But I'll tell you. Lots of folks in this world ain't had that
much! Well, good mornin'.

MATHILDA

Mornin'. Sorry you won't stay.

[UNCLE WALTER *is out the front door.* MATHILDA *speaks in
a loud clear voice to no one in particular.*]

MATHILDA

Seems a shame, a downright shame, all this good cookin' goin' to waste!

[MATHILDA *turns and marches off* L. JONATHAN *follows her. The Gage family indulge in a long, thoughtful pause.*]

SARAH

Mother.

MARGE

Yes, dear?

SARAH [*rising and crossing* L]

I wonder if you would excuse me.

HERBERT

Where are you going?

SARAH [*starting toward the bedroom,* L]

I think I left my—[*She runs off into the bedroom, slamming the door after her.*]—my scarf in with Aunt Mathilda.

[SARAH *is out* L. PAULA *starts forward on the bench.*]

HERBERT [*rising, crossing* L *one step*]

Sarah! [*He turns* R, *bitterly.*] Benedict Arnold!

MARGE [*crossing to* HERBERT]

Herbert, you can't blame the child—after all———

HERBERT [*sternly*]

Marge!

MARGE

Yes, Herbert. [*She crosses* L *and sits meekly on the sofa.*]
Well, I'm glad that one of us will survive to talk to the
newspaper men.

HERBERT [*crossing* L, *to the desk*]

Don't be silly. Missing just a meal never hurt anybody.

MARGE

It isn't just a meal. It's Sunday breakfast. And you can hardly
call what we nibbled at last night—dinner.

HERBERT

Let's not discuss it! Shall we?

[JONATHAN *opens the door* L.]

JONATHAN

You folks don't mind if I leave this door open for a spell?
Getting too blame hot in here.

[JONATHAN *retreats out* L. MARGE *crosses* L, *to the door.*]

MARGE [*standing above the sofa with her back to the open
door*]

Paula, come here. Heavens, I can just feel the heat rolling
into this room.

[PAULA *crosses down to left of* MARGE.]

PAULA

Gee, that feels good.

HERBERT

I don't believe you can feel a thing.

MARGE

Come over and see!

HERBERT [*starting to cross* L]

It's all your imagination.

[*The piano begins to peal, "Abide with Me."* JONATHAN
appears at the door L.]

JONATHAN

Know how that piano disturbs you folks. I'll just close the
door. [*He closes the door.*]

MARGE

Mr. Rockwood, we don't mind——

HERBERT

Marge! That piano does disturb us!

[*The piano stops. There is silence.* MARGE *is taking long
deep breaths.* HERBERT *is sitting on the desk.*]

HERBERT

What are you doing?

MARGE

Urnm—smell that fried ham . . .

PAULA [*sniffing*]

That's bacon!

MARGE

It's the ham I smell—the fried ham . . .

[*Suddenly,* MARGE *crosses to* HERBERT *and kisses him.* PAULA
crosses to the chair right of the sofa.]

HERBERT

Marge, what the——

MARGE

Herbert, I love you. [*She crosses to the door* L *and stops.*]
Remember that. I love you.

[MARGE *turns away from him, and walks straight into the
Rockwoods' room. She closes the door.*]

HERBERT

You won't desert your father, will you, Paula?

[HERBERT *and* PAULA *cross* R.]

PAULA

No, sir! I'll die first! [*She thinks that over, and then faces
front.*] Will you bury me under the big tree?

HERBERT [*taking the jar of olives and putting it in the box*]
Now, don't get morbid. [*He sits upstage of the table.*]

PAULA

I'm not morbid, I'm starving.

HERBERT

Sit down. Have your breakfast.

[PAULA *sits left of the table.* HERBERT *pours out corn flakes
into a bowl and sprinkles a few olives over them. Then he
pours molasses over it. He can't bear the sight and covers the
bowl with a napkin.*]

HERBERT [*rising*]
You go in Paula. Go ahead.

PAULA [*rising*]
   No! We can't let ourselves get obligated.

HERBERT [*hopefully*]
   Paula, would you feel better about going in there if Father
   went with you?

PAULA
   I couldn't let you do that just for my sake.

HERBERT
   Oh! [*He pauses—then:*] Paula, I had great plans for you.
   [*He crosses* U L *with* PAULA.] I've seen you as a great
   artist—or a journalist. I even saw you in the White House.
   The first woman president in our history.

PAULA
   I don't know if my husband would let me be president.

HERBERT
   It's warm in the White House. And you get three meals a
   day in the White House.

PAULA
   No, sir!

HERBERT
   Paula, do you want people to say I don't look out for my
   children?

PAULA
   Well, Father, if you insist . . .

HERBERT
   I do, Paula.

[PAULA *goes out* L *and slams the door in* HERBERT'S *face.* HERBERT *leans dejectedly against the back of the chair right of the sofa.* MATHILDA *opens the door* L.]

MATHILDA

Mr. Gage.

HERBERT

Yes?

MATHILDA

Wouldn't you like a nice cup of hot coffee?

HERBERT

No, thanks. I've just had some corn flakes.

[MATHILDA *starts to close the door.* HERBERT *hesitates a second, and then rushes into the bedroom after* MATHILDA. *In a moment,* BARBARA *and* MATT *enter* R. MATT *drops the suitcase.* BARBARA *shushes him.*]

BARBARA

Quiet, Matt. Everybody's still in bed.

MATT [*pointing to the table*]

They must have had a late snack before retiring last night.

BARBARA

Yes. [*She lifts the napkin and sees the dish her father concocted—corn flakes, olives, and molasses.*] No wonder they're still in bed.

[MATT *crosses* L, *below* BARBARA, *to* C.]

BARBARA

Matt, I'm so tired, I can't see. [*She sits in the chair right of the desk.*]

MATT

You had a busy time of it. [*He crosses* L *and hangs his coat on a peg.*]

BARBARA

When Mrs. Tuttle trudged in this morning, I could have kissed her.

MATT

You did kiss her.

BARBARA

Did I? I was out on my feet.

MATT [*crossing* R, *to left of the desk*]

She said you did a good job of it.

BARBARA

We did a good job, Matt.

MATT

No, it was you. All I did was hot water. Women sure have it tough. [*He sits on the desk.*]

BARBARA [*with a rush*]

Matt, I was scared to death! When I held that tiny thing up by its heels, I was afraid to hit it! I couldn't—it didn't seem fair—and then I did, and it began to yell. [*She sinks back in the chair.*] Matt, when I get married, I'm going to deliver all my own babies—every single one.

MATT

Mrs. Gorley says she's going to name it after you.

BARBARA

But it's a boy!

MATT

Mrs. Gorley says she doesn't care.

BARBARA [laughing, rising]

I'll put a stop to that. We'll call it Matt.

MATT

Matt . . . [He likes that.] Matthew Gorley. [He smiles.]

BARBARA [crossing L, to the pegs, taking off her coat]

Well, I'm going to bed. I don't think I can sleep, but I'm going to try.

MATT [rising, crossing L]

Me, too. Think your father will be mad? About the car?

BARBARA

We'll go back this afternoon and dig it out.

MATT

If I'm still asleep when you're ready to go, wake me.

BARBARA [on the stairs]

I hope Mrs. Tuttle keeps my baby covered.

MATT

Say, Barbara—you think your father knows anybody that could get me a Social Security card?

[BARBARA has gone up the stairs, and MATT follows. In a moment, the Rockwoods' door, L, opens. MATHILDA and MARGE enter, chatting cozily.]

MARGE

Mrs. Rockwood, your strawberry preserves are wonderful, simply wonderful!

[MATHILDA *and* MARGE *sit on the sofa.*]

MATHILDA [*shaking her head*]
No—had bad luck with them this year.

MARGE
I don't see how you cook at all on that wood stove of yours.

MATHILDA
Couldn't cook on any other stove.

MARGE
Children!

[SARAH *and* PAULA *drift in* L, *nibbling biscuits.*]

MARGE
How do you like those biscuits, children?

SARAH [*leaning over the back of the sofa and putting her cheek against* MATILDA'S]
Oh, they're divine, Aunt Mathilda. Divine!

MARGE
Paula?

[PAULA *is leaning against the chair right of the sofa, her mouth so full she has trouble admitting the biscuits are good.*]

PAULA
Not bad. Not bad at all.

MARGE
Mrs. Rockwood, how do you keep your canned things from exploding?

MATHILDA

I don't see how you get yours *to* explode!

MARGE [*laughing*]

Oh, it's easy! I'll show you.

[JONATHAN *enters* L *and crosses* R, *to the fireplace, with an armful of wood.*]

MARGE

That's awfully nice of you, Mr. Rockwood.

JONATHAN

Ain't done nothin' yet.

[PAULA *crosses* R, *to* JONATHAN, *and sits on the bench.* SARAH *crosses up and sits on the window seat.*]

MARGE

I don't know what it is about Herbert—where there's smoke there's supposed to be fire. But not *Herbert's* smoke!

[HERBERT *walks in from the bedroom,* L. *He is lighting a pipe, taking that first delightful drag after a heavy, satisfying meal, inhaling deeply. He loosens his belt. He crosses* R, *to the chair left of the table, and sits, putting his foot on the stool and watching* JONATHAN *fix the fire.*]

HERBERT [*suddenly*]

Rockwood, I've been thinking. Have we got room out in the barn for five or six more pigs?

JONATHAN [*rising*]

Plenty o' room.

HERBERT

And what about a bull?

JONATHAN [*bending down to fix the fire*]

Bulls can be mean. Never like a bull 'round where there's children.

HERBERT [*rising*]

Rockwood—uh—you know, with the damn electricity out—— [*He stops and turns to* MATHILDA.] Excuse me, Mrs. Rockwood. [*He turns to* JONATHAN, *speaking in a low voice.*] With the electricity out . . . [*He looks upstairs.*]

JONATHAN

Know what's on your mind. Go right ahead.

HERBERT

Thanks a lot.

[HERBERT *goes out the front door.* JONATHAN *crosses up* L, *gets the Coolidge picture, and places it on the desk (or hangs it on the wall).*]

MARGE

Mrs. Rockwood, you must give me the recipe for your strawberry preserves.

MATHILDA

No need to give you the recipe. I'll give you the preserves.

[JONATHAN *has finished setting up the Coolidge picture and turns to* MARGE *for her reaction. She smiles graciously.*]

MARGE

A fine-looking man, wasn't he?

JONATHAN

Wouldn't go so far as to say that. [*He crosses down and sits in the chair right of the sofa.*]

MARGE

Mr. Rockwood. I'm sorry about everything—the way everything has been. But when people are crowded together like
we've all been—well, there's bound to be some misunder-
standings. And I want to explain to you. I know how much
this house means to you, but we love it, too. And besides all
that, we've spent a lot of money fixing it up, and we
couldn't afford to leave it—even if we wanted to.

JONATHAN

How much it cost you to spoil this house?

MARGE

Nearly eight thousand dollars.

JONATHAN

Eight thousand! Hmm. Take pretty near that to get it back in
shape again.

MARGE

But we like it the way it is!

MATHILDA

Different folks has different tastes, Jonathan.

JONATHAN

Ain't a question of taste. It's all these modern inconven-
iences!

MATHILDA

Some of them are real practical.

JONATHAN

Mighty few. Maybe indoor plumbin'—if it ain't too ex-
pensive. [*He turns to* MARGE.] And that reminds me. I'd

like to put a word in for the barn before you take it into your head to do any improvin' out there.

MATHILDA

Jonathan, what are you thinkin'?

JONATHAN

Been in the back of my mind for quite a spell.

MATHILDA

Jonathan! Folks don't live in barns!

JONATHAN

Don't eh? What 'bout the Fergusons? After their house burned down? Helped Ferguson remodel his barn, and I done such a good job they're still livin' in it. Like it. Them old stone barns was built better than the houses. And our barn is older than the Fergusons'.

MARGE

It is?

JONATHAN

Yep. Barn of ours is the oldest buildin' in this part of the state. [*He turns to* MATHILDA.] Heard your grandpop say so many a time. It was put up—forty years before this house was. First house burned down.

MARGE [*rising, crossing* R, *very interested*]

You mean, our barn is older than this house?

JONATHAN

Yep. And the barn's always cool in the summer, comfortable in winter.

MATHILDA

You're the head of the family, Jonathan.

JONATHAN

Can't start diggin' the cellar till the ground softens.

[HERBERT *enters at the front door, holding a page torn out of a mail-order catalogue.*]

HERBERT

Listen, Rockwood. If we could get one of these deluxe hand cultivators, then next spring we could make your garden twice as big, and we could make mine into a tennis court.

JONATHAN [*nodding*]

Your garden would make a good tennis court now.

MARGE [*crossing* L, *to* HERBERT]

Herbert, do you know that our barn is the oldest building in Connecticut?

HERBERT

Really?

MARGE

Yes! It's forty years older than this house! Herbert, I never realized the barn's possibilities! It would be charming!

HERBERT

Charming!

MARGE

We could have a studio living-room—you know—two stories high—and a staircase to a balcony, with our bedrooms off it—that would be where the haymow is now, and——

HERBERT

Our bedrooms? What are you——

MARGE

It'd be cool in summer and comfortable in winter!

HERBERT

Now, wait a minute, Marge!

JONATHAN

Yep, hold on, Mrs. Gage. It's Mathilda and me that——

MARGE

Oh, no! I'm sorry, Mr. Rockwood, there wouldn't be room for us all in the barn. It's too crowded. I'm afraid you will have to stay in the house.

HERBERT

Marge, what——

MARGE

Herbert, just think how wonderful it would be! The fun! And we'd have the oldest house in Connecticut!

HERBERT

Listen! Be practical, darling, be practical!

MARGE

I am! Barbara wouldn't have to double up with Sarah, and——[*She stops.*] Barbara! [*She pauses and crosses* L, *to right of the chair right of the sofa.*] Mr. Rockwood, Mrs. Rockwood, what do you think about Barbara and Matt? Really, I mean?

JONATHAN

To tell you the truth, I don't approve of this intermarriage business.

MARGE

Intermarriage? What in the world do you mean?

JONATHAN

Democrats should marry Democrats.

HERBERT [crossing up to the stairs]

I don't want to discuss politics with you . . .

[BARBARA is coming down the stairs. She has changed into pajamas and a robe.]

BARBARA [gaily]

Good morning! Everybody!

MARGE [crossing up to left of the stairs]

Barbara!

[HERBERT is right of the stairs.]

BARBARA

Good morning, Mother!

MARGE

Darling, what are you doing here?

BARBARA [laughing]

I live here. Remember?

HERBERT

Barbara, where have you been?

BARBARA

I thought you knew. Last night, Mrs. Gorley's baby came sooner than expected, and Matt and I helped deliver it. [*She crosses* R, *below* HERBERT.]

HERBERT

Are you and Matt married?

BARBARA

Married! [*Her hands are on* HERBERT'S *shoulders, and she laughs.*] Don't be silly.

[BARBARA *sees* MATT *on the stairs.*]

BARBARA

Matt, tell them—are we married?

MATT

Married? No. What——

HERBERT [*going to him*]

You aren't?

MATT

Of course not!

HERBERT [*shaking hands heartily with* MATT]

How are you, Matt? Glad to see you.

MATT [*amazed*]

Glad to see me?

MARGE [*crossing* R, *below* HERBERT]

Barbara, why in the world didn't you tell us about Mrs. Gorley! Good Heavens! George! Poor George!

BARBARA [*fearing the worst*]
Mother! What about George?

MARGE
He was here! He just got out of college. But when he discovered you had eloped with Matt, he———

BARBARA
Eloped! How could George think that—how could he?

MARGE
There was nothing else to think, dear.

BARBARA
Where is George?

MARGE
He's gone.

HERBERT
Our car! Barbara, maybe we can catch him on the parkway.

BARBARA
Our car's back at Gorleys'! Stuck!

[BARBARA *leans against the desk.* MARGE'S *arm is around* BARBARA'S *shoulder.*]

BARBARA
Oh, Mother!

MARGE
Now, now, dear.

[CARSON *steps inside the front door without knocking.*]

CARSON
Well, folks, good morning again.

[MATT *crosses to* L C.]

HERBERT

Oh, it's you.

CARSON

Yes, I run into something. I think I got a clue as to your daughter's whereabouts.

HERBERT

Really? Congratulations!

CARSON [*pulling a photograph out of his pocket*]
This your daughter? [*He hands the picture to* MARGE.]

HERBERT

There's our daughter right there!

CARSON

Say, I've been looking all over for you.

MARGE

That isn't the picture I gave you. Where did you get that?

CARSON [*crossing to the mantel, replacing the photo on the mantel*]
Well, I'll tell you. I stopped back at Headquarters after I left here, and one of the boys had a fellow there he picked up for reckless driving. Among the fellow's credentials I found this picture of Matt Rockwood's wife. Naturally, I got suspicious.

BARBARA [*running to* CARSON]
George! I gave that picture to George!

[*A* CONSTABLE *enters at the front door with* GEORGE.]

CONSTABLE
Here he is, Carson!

BARBARA [*seeing* GEORGE]
George! [*She crosses up and throws her arms around his neck.*]

[SARAH *goes out* L *and closes the door.*]

GEORGE
Well, Mrs. Rockwood!

BARBARA
I'm not married, George. I'm not!

GEORGE [*slowly*]
You're not?

BARBARA
I went with Matt to Mrs. Gorley's. She was having a baby, and—George, I was just out on an obstetrical case!

[*The piano, off* L, *starts playing,* "Here Comes the Bride."]

HERBERT [*very charming*]
Rockwood, if I can give up swearing, I'm sure Mrs. Rockwood won't mind giving up that piano. [*He smiles at* MATHILDA.] Mathilda, would you mind not playing that——[*He looks around.*] Dammit, Sara-a-a-h! [*He starts toward the bedroom.*]

[UNCLE WALTER *rushes in the front door.*]

UNCLE WALTER
John! John! Got some news for you!

JONATHAN

That so, Uncle Walter?

UNCLE WALTER

Yep. Last night Mrs. Gorley had her baby. She ain't "expectin'" no more!

CURTAIN